FEELS SO GOOD TO LAY DOWN

40 Life Lessons
Grounded in Biblical Truths

Tiffany Haynes Vinson

Feels So Good to Lay Down
Trilogy Christian Publishers A Wholly Owned Subsidiary of Trinity Broadcasting Network
2442 Michelle Drive Tustin, CA 92780
Copyright © 2024 by Tiffany Haynes Vinson

Unless otherwise indicated, Scripture quotations are taken from the New King James Version®. Copyright © 1982 by Thomas Nelson. Used by permission. All rights reserved. Scripture quotations marked ESV are taken from the ESV® Bible (The Holy Bible, English Standard Version®), copyright © 2001 by Crossway Bibles, a publishing ministry of Good News Publishers. ©All rights reserved. Scripture quotations marked NASB are taken from the New American Standard Bible® (NASB), Copyright © 1960, 1962, 1963, 1968, 1971, 1972, 1973, 1975, 1977, 1995 by The Lockman Foundation. Used by permission. www.Lockman.org. Scripture quotations marked NIV are taken from the Holy Bible, New International Version®, NIV®. Copyright © 1973, 1978, 1984, 2011 by Biblica, Inc.™ Used by permission of Zondervan. All rights reserved worldwide. www.zondervan.com. The "NIV" and "New International Version" are trademarks registered in the United States Patent and Trademark Office by Biblica, Inc.™ Scripture quotations marked NLT are taken from the Holy Bible, New Living Translation, copyright © 1996, 2004, 2015 by Tyndale House Foundation. Used by permission of Tyndale House Publishers, Inc., Carol Stream, Illinois 60188. All rights reserved. Scripture quotations marked TLV are taken from the Holy Scriptures, Tree of Life Version*. Copyright © 2014, 2016 by the Tree of Life Bible Society. Used by permission of the Tree of Life Bible Society. Scripture quotations marked TPT are taken from The Passion Translation®. Copyright©2017, 2018, 2020 by Passion and Fire Ministries, Inc. Used by permission. All rights reserved. ThePassionTranslation.com.

No part of this book may be reproduced, stored in a retrieval system, or transmitted by any means without written permission from the author. All rights reserved. Printed in the USA.
Rights Department, 2442 Michelle Drive, Tustin, CA 92780.
Trilogy Christian Publishing/TBN and colophon are trademarks of Trinity Broadcasting Network.
For information about special discounts for bulk purchases, please contact Trilogy Christian Publishing.
Trilogy Disclaimer: The views and content expressed in this book are those of the author and may not necessarily reflect the views and doctrine of Trilogy Christian Publishing or the Trinity Broadcasting Network.

10 9 8 7 6 5 4 3 2 1
Library of Congress Cataloging-in-Publication Data is available.
ISBN: 979-8-89333-733-4
E-ISBN: 979-8-89333-734-1

To my husband, Shad:

You have given me so many memorable quotes, and you always bring things into the right perspective. I love you.

To my two boys, Clemmie and Colt:

You have given me stories to tell, and you teach me so much about the God I serve. I love you both.

Our Heavenly Father truly is faithful.

I'm thankful for each of your lives and how I'm drawn in closer to Him because of you.

May our Lord Jesus be honored and glorified in our stories, and may we never forget how good it feels to lay it all down at the end of the day.

Selah.

Psalm 3

Table of Contents

Acknowledgments. 11

Lesson 1   The Grilled Cheese by the Air Vent 13

Lesson 2   "Stop Clapping Your Poop Hands!" 17

Lesson 3   It's All a Matter of Perspective 23

Lesson 4   Swatting Flies and Heinies 29

Lesson 5   "I Want the Squeaky Shoe". 35

Lesson 6   "I Love You, but You Smell Like Hot Dogs". 39

Lesson 7   Eating the Buttons Off the Calculator. 43

Lesson 8   Mommy Twister 47

Lesson 9   "Get in Here Now!" 53

Lesson 10   "Clem, Quit Chunkin' Your Chicken!". 59

Lesson 11   "Clem, Quit Chunkin' Your Chicken!". 65

Lesson 12   "Slow Down, Mommy! I'm Spilling My Chocolate Milk!" 71

Lesson 13   Wearing Daddy's Shoes 75

Lesson 14   "Are We There Yet?". 81

Lesson 15   "Mommy, Can I Get a Puppy?" 85

Lesson 16	A Tree Planted by Streams of Water 93
Lesson 17	So Close, Yet So Far Away 99
Lesson 18	"Mom, You're Beautiful" 105
Lesson 19	My Ghost Story...................... 111
Lesson 20	The "Shade-y" Choice 121
Lesson 21	Red and Yellow, Black and White........ 129
Lesson 22	What's in a Name? 135
Lesson 23	Playing Second Fiddle 145
Lesson 24	"It's Not a Kai-Peeper!" 151
Lesson 25	That's Good Enough.................. 159
Lesson 26	Stuck Between Walls 167
Lesson 27	Pick Up Trash or Pick Flowers ... Your Choice 173
Lesson 28	"I Messed Up, Mommy! I'm No Good!" . . 181
Lesson 29	The Pathway Cleared 187
Lesson 30	"Put Him Down"..................... 193
Lesson 31	"Life Is Like a Popcorn Toot" 201
Lesson 32	Preparing the Soil 207
Lesson 33	He Does More....................... 217
Lesson 34	"Don't Drop the Fruit" 229

Lesson 35	Brother's Keeper	237
Lesson 36	Overlooking the Heart of God	247
Lesson 37	The Joy of Disentanglement	263
Lesson 38	Growth Spurts	271
Lesson 39	A "Chord" of Three Strands	281
Lesson 40	Why the Delay?	291
Afterword	Glossary of Transliterations	311
About the Author		315

Acknowledgments

When a work has been twenty years in the making, there are many people who bring something to the table. I am eternally grateful for my parents, Ed and Sandy Haynes, who taught me about Jesus from the time I entered this world to the present. They are the reason I have a passion for Scripture and a deep love for Jesus. It is because of their steadfast commitment to the Lord that I committed my life to Him. Thank you, Mom and Dad, and thank you for helping with Clemmie while I finished this book. To my two precious sisters, Tonya and Tara, thank you both for times of correction, times of comfort, and everything in between. I am so thankful God made us a three-stranded "chord," and I desire to sing His praises with you until He takes us home. I am also grateful for the many women, from California to Oklahoma to Maryland, who have inspired me to dive deep into the Word. I have fasted with you, prayed with you, and studied with you in order to lean in close to my Savior so that I may be able to hear His heartbeat. To my new Texas neighbors and friends, I look forward to growing more with you. Be gracious and patient with me as I continue to raise up two young men in the fear and love of the Lord, as the Holy Spirit gives wisdom. Thank you, Trilogy Publishing and Stacy, for trusting me to write a book worthy for others to read. Shad, my heart is filled with gratitude for you and our boys. You have been my constant encouragement and unending support for twenty-seven years. *Ich liebe dich.* To my Lord and Savior, Jesus, thank You for these words. May they bring encouragement and understanding to all who read them. I love You.

LESSON 1

The Grilled Cheese by the Air Vent

Psalm 37:4–9; Psalm 130:5; Isaiah 40:31;
Galatians 5:22–23; James 1:4

The Lord is good to those who wait for Him, to the soul who seeks Him. It is good that one should hope and wait quietly for the salvation of the Lord.
—**Lamentations 3:25–26**

But let patience have its perfect work, that you may be perfect and complete, lacking nothing.
—**James 1:4**

It was a hot summer day in Texas when my sister Tara and I decided to load the kids up in her minivan for a trip to Sonic. The kids, four in total, were so excited. They were craving corn dogs, chicken strips, fries, watermelon slushes, and grilled cheese sandwiches. We pulled into the first spot available and placed the order. With the smell of fries in the air, the anticipation grew stronger as we waited for the food to be delivered to the car. "Mom, when will the food be here?" You would've thought they were starving! The food arrived in about ten minutes' time, fresh out of the oven. After we had handed each child's particular food item to them, they began munching away . . . that is, everyone but the child who had ordered the grilled cheese sandwich! Tara noticed how hot the sandwich was when she took it out of the bag, so she held on to it to give it time to cool. "Mom! I'm hungry! I want my grilled cheese sandwich now!" The "famished" child evidently could *not* wait any longer, but *Mommy* knew better. Tara and I began to problem-solve as mommies learn to do. How could we cool this sandwich quickly? Why not put it in front of the air vent where we had the most frigid air blowing on that hot Texas summer day?! Well, that's exactly what we did, and after about five minutes, the grilled cheese sandwich was ready to eat. All was well in our little world again.

In this "fast food" society, we have become a people who no longer know how to wait. We want it *now*, on our own timeline, and we feel as though we won't survive without it right when we want it. Probably the better lesson we've could've taught our kids in that moment would've been the value in letting the grilled cheese cool on its own. Because we were in such a rush to cool it down next to the air vent, the outside temperature of the sandwich might've been vastly different from the inside, making it deceptively seem ready to eat. That first bite might not have burned the mouth, but the second bite—ouch! Or our rush to cool it down and appease the appetite for instant tummy gratification could have resulted in a very cold sandwich instead of a perfectly warm and gooey grilled cheese. Either way, the sandwich might not have been experienced in its very best form, leaving an unsatisfied partaker or one who only ultimately expects the mediocre. "But those who wait on the LORD shall renew their strength; they shall mount up with wings like eagles, they shall run and not be weary, they shall walk and not faint" (Isaiah 40:31).

Sometimes we work ourselves into a tizzy trying to speed up the process of attaining what we want! Our awesome and faithful heavenly Father knows best. He knows the *when*, the *where*, and the *how* to give us the desires of our heart . . . if those desires are for our good and *His* glory. As we mature in holy faith, may our desires line up with His, and may we be a people who are long-suffering and exude patience, in Jesus' name. May we be a people who expect the very best meal from our heavenly Father—which is always worth the wait! "But I—I will watch for ADONAI. I will wait for the God of my salvation. My God will hear me" (Micah 7:7 TLV).

Revelation: Learn patience and wait while God works all things for our good. It's all about His timing, not ours; otherwise, we could get burned.

FEELS SO GOOD TO LAY DOWN

WRITE DOWN WHAT THE HOLY SPIRIT SAYS TO YOU:

LESSON 2

"Stop Clapping Your Poop Hands!"

2 Samuel 22:4; 1 Chronicles 16:35; 2 Chronicles 20:22;
Psalm 34:1; Psalm 98:8; Psalm 118:24; Psalm 150:6;
John 16:33; Philippians 4:4; 1 Peter 1:3–7

> *Oh, clap your hands, all you peoples! Shout to God with the voice of triumph!*
> **—Psalm 47:1**

> *But you are a chosen generation, a royal priesthood, a holy nation, His own special people, that you may proclaim the praises of Him who called you out of darkness into His marvelous light.*
> **—1 Peter 2:9**

It was our first long road trip after we'd had our second son. We were traveling from where we lived in Maryland to our home state of Texas to visit family. Our newest addition was quite content in the back seat of our Suburban with his big brother, but my husband and I started to get wind of something terrible that had apparently erupted. The strong malodorous scent began to fill the cabin of our vehicle. We knew who the culprit of origin might be, so we pulled the car into a spot at a Sonic Drive-In somewhere in Virginia (we like Sonic!). My husband, being the "take charge" guy that he is, was the first to get out, and before I could get out to open the door of access to the stinky backseat passenger, Daddy was ready to take care of business. He found out *really* quick that our then-six-month-old child had filled his diaper to full capacity—and beyond. Now, usually babies get really irritable and uncomfortable when they've just messed their britches, but not our second-born. He seemed to revel in it! Not only that, but he was so excited to be out of that car seat and see his daddy's face that his body began to squirm, and his hands went right into the mess he had just created. Daddy's face began to turn beet-red, and steam started coming out of his ears.

This seemed to only cause this little bundle of joy to celebrate more, and he began to clap his little hands as his daddy tried to clean him up. Daddy then exclaimed, "Stop clapping your poop hands!" Needless to say, this story has become a source of laughter for all of us now, but at the time of the "dirty job," we were too focused on the mess to appreciate the joyful little dude who was feeling really good at that moment. We adults tend to do that. We focus on the problem instead of the Problem Fixer. And while we're focusing on the problem, we discourage others from praising God in the midst of the problem. Scripture tells us in Psalm 8:2 (NIV) that "through the praise of children and infants you have established a stronghold against your enemies, to silence the foe and the avenger." Why in the world would we want to hinder the praise of our children when their praises shut the enemy's mouth? Our little guy was so happy that he had his daddy's attention, that he was set free from his car seat for a moment, and that he had just unloaded into his diaper *everything* that was causing him discomfort. He was rejoicing!

Do you know that you have your heavenly Father's complete attention (Matthew 6:8)? Do you know that you have been set free through Jesus Christ (Romans 8:2)? Do you know that all your stinky mess was unloaded upon Jesus at the cross at Calvary (2 Corinthians 5:21)? Beloved, we also have so much to rejoice about!

Truly knowing God—the Father, the Son, and the Holy Spirit—means understanding that He alone can create a message out of our mess. He alone can take a test and make it a testimony. *He* is the One who cleans us up and gets rid of the stink. Therefore, we must "walk in love, as Christ also has loved us and given Himself for us, an offering and a sacrifice to God for a sweet-smelling aroma" (Ephesians 5:2). And, yes, even after we've been cleaned up, we can rejoice, with childlike faith, that our Abba is faithful to continue the work in cleaning us up through the Holy Spirit (Philippians 1:6). He never gives up on His children. Praise the Lord! "Though your sins be like scarlet, they will be as white as snow" (Isaiah 1:18 TLV). Jesus' precious atoning blood has accomplished everything that needed to be done to make us clean. Our Lord Jesus Christ is so worthy to be praised. Have you been set free? Have you been made clean? It's time to rejoice! "Lift up your hands in the sanctuary and bless the LORD" (Psalm 134:2)!

Revelation: Praise our God despite the mess. Don't focus on the problem, but rather on the Problem-Solver!

"STOP CLAPPING YOUR POOP HANDS!"

WRITE DOWN WHAT THE HOLY SPIRIT SAYS TO YOU:

_____

_____

_____

_____

_____

_____

_____

_____

_____

_____

_____

_____

_____

_____

_____

_____

_____

_____

_____

_____

LESSON 3

It's All a Matter of Perspective

Proverbs 27:5–6; Matthew 6:34;
Romans 5:1–5; Jude 1:16–25

A merry heart does good, like medicine, but a broken spirit dries the bones.
—**Proverbs 17:22**

Now may the God of hope fill you with all joy and peace in believing, that you may abound in hope by the power of the Holy Spirit.
—**Romans 15:13**

Have you known people, no matter what good is going on in their life, who always seem to focus on the bad? I'm reminded of how selfish we can be at times. Though clothed, fed, and housed, we seem to never be content. I believe it's all a matter of perspective.

My oldest son, Clemmie (whom you'll continue to read more about), was diagnosed with a rare genetic disorder at seven and a half months old. He had seizures for the first ten years of his life . . . *every* day, *several times* a day. His whole life has been filled with memories of MRIs, CT scans, EEGs, and blood tests. He has grown so accustomed to these doctors' visits that now, at twenty years old, he handles all of it *extremely* well. In fact, he smiles and laughs through the appointments most of the time. When Mommy and Daddy seem a little stressed, he usually gets right in our face, smiles, and then makes a toot noise with his mouth ("boy moms" will understand). He knows how to break the ice, and he wants us to be just as joyful as he is in that moment. He is absolutely a gift!

What if we all were to be a little bit more like Clemmie and thankful for our lives? What if we were to live life like we were "called . . . out of darkness into His marvelous light" (1 Peter 2:9)? From Genesis to Revelation, almighty God has proven His faithfulness time and time again, and yet His people consistently seem to forget His mighty acts of provision and deliverance. He would rescue them, and they would find themselves again enslaved because of their lack of contentment in the God who provides, YHWH-Jireh (Genesis 22:14). The grass always seems a little greener on the other side of the fence, doesn't it? Is it really, or is the way we see things a little skewed?

Psalm 107 begins with an emphatic statement that should be on display in the life of every born-again believer: "Oh, give thanks to the LORD, for He is good! For His mercy endures forever. Let the redeemed of the LORD say so." Scripture never tells the redeemed of the Lord to make sure everyone knows how bad things are and focus on the troubles of this world. "Rejoice in the Lord always. Again I will say, rejoice!" (Philippians 4:4). Yes, the troubles are many, especially for the people of God whom Satan sees as a threat to his agenda, but God! In John 16:33 (TPT), Jesus reminds us that "everything I've taught you is so that the peace which is in me will be in you and will give you great confidence as you rest in me. For in this unbelieving world you will experience trouble and sorrows, but you must be courageous, for I have conquered the world." Do we actually believe that "we are more than conquerors" because of Jesus and His great love for us (Romans 8:37)? To be *redeemed* means to be *bought back into kinship* with the Great I Am. That is Good News—and more than enough to rejoice about! So, why not proclaim that Good News?

The Israelites were set free from oppression time and time again. Yet they continued to forget how they had been set free from bondage because they took their eyes off their Deliverer, their *Shalom*, and focused instead on their troubles. They lacked contentment in His provision and selfishly kept going back to what had enslaved them in the first place. They lacked peace in YHWH-Shalom, in whom they could find rest in their striving, prosperity in their wanting, and quietness in their turmoil. They lacked

His peace, not because He wasn't there to provide that peace, but because they continuously lost sight of their God's faithfulness and character. They saw things from the bottom of the valley instead of the top of the mountain. They were ungrateful and lived as victims instead of victors. They lacked the right perspective. Fleshly desires, and taking our eyes off Jesus, the Author and Perfecter of our faith, will always lead us back to the darkness from which we were pulled. "Oh, that men would give thanks to the LORD for His goodness, and for His wonderful works to the children of men!" (Psalm 107:8, 15, 21, 31).

Daniel Clemmie has the right perspective and understands better than most "how wide, how long, how high, and how deep" the love of our Father is for us (Ephesians 3:18). He is thankful, and he reminds us every day in whom he places his trust. "But He lifts the needy high above affliction and makes their families like a flock. The upright see it and are glad, and all iniquity shuts its mouth. Who is wise? Let him observe these things, and consider ADONAI's lovingkindness" (Psalm 107:41–43). Can you imagine how much more abundant life would be if we *saw* everything with thankful hearts and considered our God's lovingkindness? It's all a matter of perspective. May we see things through eyes of faith in what Jesus has already done for all who trust in His promises and be thankful.

Revelation: Contentment in Christ Jesus, and a grateful heart for what He has already done, will keep us focused more on Him and less on ourselves. How we see things will be proof of our gratitude.

WRITE DOWN WHAT THE HOLY SPIRIT SAYS TO YOU:

LESSON 4

Swatting Flies and Heinies

Deuteronomy 8:5; Proverbs 4; Proverbs 12:15; Proverbs 19:20–21; Proverbs 27:5–6; Matthew 7:11; Hebrews 12:7; Revelation 3:19

My child, don't reject the LORD's discipline, and don't be upset when he corrects you. For the LORD corrects those he loves, just as a father corrects a child in whom he delights.
—Proverbs 3:11–12 NLT

All Scripture is given by inspiration of God, and is profitable for doctrine, for reproof, for correction, for instruction in righteousness.
—2 Timothy 3:16

Who would've thought that a flyswatter could be analogous to the Word of God? I'm very thankful that both my boys are very good to receive correction when they need it. We've tried to instill in them not only to apologize for bad behavior, but to be repentant and change their behavior when needed. My youngest, Colt, has always been aware of the extraordinary situation our family is in with my oldest son's diagnosis. The Lord knew I would need a very agreeable and kind child to be a helper and not feel neglected in times of medical tests and health emergencies. I am exceedingly grateful for that. However, one day Colt needed to be physically disciplined for bad behavior. He was disobeying me while I happened to have my flyswatter out, ready to kill some annoying insects. At that moment the flyswatter was the "rod" (Proverbs 13:24) I used to correct my son. Yes, it stung his little bottom, and, yes it hurt his pride, but he needed an immediate correction. Hebrews 12:11 (TLV) says, "Now all discipline seems painful at the moment—not joyful. But later it yields the peaceful fruit of righteousness to those who have been trained by it." Wouldn't we all prefer the "peaceful fruit of righteousness" in our children—and in us? Better to start early than wait for the more severe lessons that might need to be learned. After I spanked him, I turned around and got rid of those pesky flies that had been aggravating us. The flyswatter became a "two-edged sword" for my son. It reminded him of his disobedience, and the punishment that came with that disobedience, and then, hopefully, it helped to change his mind about future disobedience. At the same time, it got rid of those irritating flies, which made our home a more pleasant place to live. Isn't that like the Word of God? It corrects, yet comforts (Psalm 23:4). It divides, yet restores (Hebrews 4:12). It is a weapon of warfare, yet it heals (Ephesians 6:17; Psalm 107:20). It reveals the sin, yet brings the Good News of salvation.

At the moment of correction, and immediately afterward, my son had a choice to make. Would he receive or reject my discipline? Was he going to become grateful or bitter? Would he be thankful for the discipline and the eradication of the flies buzzing around his food, or would he focus on the bitter sting of the spanking? Was he going to choose humility and correction leading to life abundant and full of blessings, or would he choose pride and self-pity? "God opposes the proud, but gives grace to the humble" (James 4:6).

The Bible is very clear about the importance of instruction and correction, especially to the believer. If we truly believe we are an imperfect people, then we should always be willing to receive correction in our lives. Sometimes God will speak to us directly, and sometimes He will bring others into our lives to bring correction. "He who keeps instruction is in the way of life, but he who refuses correction goes astray" (Proverbs 10:17). I am a rule follower, and I never wanted to disappoint my parents, or my Jesus. When I needed correction and discipline, I would receive it and correct my behavior. I even remember being corrected by church members at times. I would quietly agree and change what I was doing. I simply did not have a rebellious spirit, but as a child, I still required correction and discipline at times.

The Scriptures talk about "foolishness [being] bound up in the heart of a child" (Proverbs 22:15). We are all born with a sin nature that separates us from almighty God and His righteousness. I don't care who you are, we are all in need of correction. The sooner we learn to receive instruction, the better instruments we will be for His glory. The problem with most of us receiving admonishment and correction is that we lack the humility. "Let nothing be done through selfish ambition or conceit, but in lowliness of mind let each esteem others better than himself" (Philippians 2:3). Sure, many will say things that make them *seem* humble. We have gotten really good at false humility. How do we treat others, though? Is there proof in our lives that we truly "esteem others better than" ourselves? Are we willing to gracefully receive correction from anyone the Spirit wills?

The mark of a Christian, just as it was in Jesus, is humility. I believe Jesus fasted and prayed so that His flesh would submit to the authority and clear instruction from the Father. He was sinless. We are not, so how much more do we need the Holy Spirit's instruction in our lives? Second Timothy 3:17 says, "God uses it to prepare and equip his people to do every good work" (NLT). The Passion Translation puts it this way, "Then you will be God's servant, fully mature and perfectly prepared to fulfill any assignment God gives you." How many of us want to be "fully mature and perfectly prepared" to do all that God has called us to do? I know I do!

I still receive correction and admonishment from those in my life who live fruit-filled, godly lives. I've even had some people I do not know issue words of caution when the Spirit leads them to do so. I would like to think it is because they discern a teachable spirit in me. I pray so. Of course, I test their "word of knowledge" against the Word (1 John 4:1). The Word of God is that "two-edged sword." If we let it divide the ugly from our lives, through the life-giving power of the Holy Spirit, the result can be a beautiful picture of maturity in Jesus Christ for all the world to see. Lord, may we be humble to receive correction however You send it, in Jesus' name.

Revelation: Discipline protects from harm. The same hand that disciplines also protects. Trust God to set boundaries for your safety and for your good!

FEELS SO GOOD TO LAY DOWN

WRITE DOWN WHAT
THE HOLY SPIRIT SAYS TO YOU:

LESSON 5

"I Want the Squeaky Shoe"

Matthew 23:11; Mark 10:45; Luke 6:31; Romans 12:9–10;
1 Corinthians 10:24; Ephesians 5:21;
Philippians 2:3; James 3:16

> *Haughtiness goes before destruction;*
> *humility precedes honor.*
> **—Proverbs 18:12** NLT

> *Let nothing be done through selfish ambition or conceit, but in lowliness of mind let each esteem others better than himself. Let each of you look out not only for his own interests, but also for the interests of others.*
> **—Philippians 2:3–4**

Unlike my two sisters and me, who were born within a total of three and a half years of each other, my two boys were born almost six years apart. This kind of age difference, mixed with the extraordinary battles my oldest son has faced, dramatically lessens any bickering and fighting between the two brothers. Clemmie sees Colt as his biggest ally, and Colt's desire is to help with Clemmie's needs. Shouldn't we all be so kind to our brothers and sisters? Shad and I have also been vigilant in making sure any signs of self-pity or jealousy are immediately squelched.

I remember when we were living in Maryland and had just bought both boys bicycles (Clemmie's was actually a trike with "big boy" training wheels). Our driveway had a pretty steep decline that went down to our house, so the boys stayed at the most level area closest to the garage. They were riding their bikes in a big circle, one after the other. At one point, Colt's competitive juices kicked in, and he loudly exclaimed, "Me first!" He rushed to get ahead of Clemmie, who was not the least bit bothered by Colt wanting to be first. Clem simply smiled and let him pass. What a perfect picture of how Christ-followers should respond to those who lack maturity in the Spirit or who might not be saved at all. Respond with grace and let them "be first." More times than not, however, we find ourselves in close relationships where competition demands first place. Jealousy demands the attention, and pride demands the award. That is human nature.

Colt has a very close relationship with each of his cousins. He *loves* spending time with them, especially the cousins who are closest to his age group. Inevitably, though, the cousin time he looks most forward to has its "me first" moments. One such instance happened when the kids were around four and five years old. All was well until we began hearing shouts coming from the other room: "I want the squeaky shoe!" Upon entering the playroom, we saw them playing tug-of-war with one shoe. What was so special about this one shoe? Well, this one shoe made a squeaky noise when you wore it. A squeaky shoe? Really? Who would want annoying, squeaky footwear? Why not want the shoe that doesn't squeak? It was clear that neither was willing to concede, so we mommies had to step in. The solution was that no one got anything. Both shoes were taken away. Everyone loses when no one wants to be gracious. Everyone loses when no one chooses humility and putting the other's needs above their own. No one gets the squeaky shoe. It's only when one person chooses to give to another that we see a reflection of what Jesus did for us. That is when we are victorious. After all, God came to earth wrapping Himself in human flesh, *humbling* Himself, "taking the very nature of a servant" (Philippians 2:7), putting our needs before His own, and ultimately taking all our punishment on the cross at Calvary. Following His perfect example of elevating others before oneself should be the goal of every born-again believer. Only then will we lead others to Him for His honor and glory.

Revelation: Put others first and align your desires with God's desires.

FEELS SO GOOD TO LAY DOWN

WRITE DOWN WHAT THE HOLY SPIRIT SAYS TO YOU:

LESSON 6

"I Love You, but You Smell Like Hot Dogs"

Romans 5:8; Romans 11:22; 1 Timothy 1:15

As dead flies cause even a bottle of perfume to stink, so a little foolishness spoils great wisdom and honor.
—**Ecclesiastes 10:1** NLT

We have all become contaminated with sin, and you see our self-righteousness as nothing better than a menstrual rag. We are all like fallen leaves, and our sins sweep us away like the wind.
—**Isaiah 64:6** TPT

And continue to walk surrendered to the extravagant love of Christ, for he surrendered his life as a sacrifice for us. His great love for us was pleasing to God, like an aroma of adoration—a sweet healing fragrance.
—**Ephesians 5:2** TPT

Summertime, with no school in session, is always a good time to spend with family. Each summer, while we were in the military, we tried to make the trip back home to Texas to get precious family time. One summer in particular we were at my sister's house having a cookout and swimming in their pool in the 100-degree Texas heat. It was a great time of fun and laughter. The hamburgers and hot dogs were plentiful, and the watermelon was cold, juicy, and sweet. It was a perfect summer day. One conversation got my attention and brought about some laughter from the family. One of the kids, who had enjoyed several hot dogs, approached her daddy with a hug. After a few sniffs, his response was, "I love you, but you smell like hot dogs!" We all laughed as she pulled away out of the initial embrace of her daddy.

At the moment, we found that interaction amusing, but aren't we thankful that our heavenly Father never turns us away from embracing Him? Though our sins be like scarlet (Isaiah 1:18), His love is so unconditional that, no matter how rotten and displeasing we are, He always welcomes us to come and abide with Him. We don't need to do the cleaning up. He cleans us up Himself and gives us a new scent through Jesus Christ. If you are His child, adopted into the Kingdom of His dear Son, then the "perfume of life" is on you. Second Corinthians 2:15, in the Passion Translation, says, "We have become the *unmistakable aroma* of the victory of the Anointed One to God—a perfume of life to those being saved and the odor of death to those who are perishing." Our pure worship is a sweet-smelling aroma to Him. "Now thanks be to God who always leads us in triumph in Christ, and through us diffuses the fragrance of His knowledge in every place" (2 Corinthians 2:14). Those who are His children, clothed in His righteousness through Jesus, bring into His presence what is sweet-smelling and beautiful. Those who do not know Jesus are perishing and have the distinct odor of death. Are we pleasing to God, or do we smell distasteful? Let me take this a bit further, if I may? How do *you* smell to others? Do you have an "*unmistakable aroma* of victory," or do you cause people to want to leave the room when you enter? Make sure today that you don't "smell like hot dogs" to the One who wants to embrace you and call you His own. May our lives emit the beautiful fragrance of a child of the Most High!

Revelation: Our heavenly Father's love for us is unfailing and unconditional—even when we stink! Allow Him to take off the stink and make you clean. "For God so loved the world that He gave His only begotten Son, that whosoever believes in Him should not perish but have everlasting life" (John 3:16).

FEELS SO GOOD TO LAY DOWN

WRITE DOWN WHAT THE HOLY SPIRIT SAYS TO YOU:

_____

_____

_____

_____

_____

_____

_____

_____

_____

_____

_____

_____

_____

_____

_____

_____

_____

_____

_____

_____

LESSON 7

Eating the Buttons Off the Calculator

Proverbs 4:23; Matthew 15:18; Mark 7:23; Luke 6:45; Galatians 6:7; Philippians 4:8; 1 Timothy 4:15

As in water face reflects face, so a man's heart reveals the man.
— **Proverbs 27:19**

"You must determine if a tree is good or rotten. You can recognize good trees by their delicious fruit. But if you find rotten fruit, you can be certain that the tree is rotten. The fruit defines the tree. But you who are known as the Pharisees are rotten to the core like venomous snakes. How can your words be good if you are rotten within? For what has been stored up in your hearts will be heard in the overflow of your words! 'When virtue is stored within, the hearts of good, upright people will produce good fruit. But when evil is hidden within, those who are

evil will produce evil fruit."
—**Matthew 12:33–35** TPT

Anyone who has ever parented a young child knows that as soon as they grab something with their hands, it immediately goes into their mouth. One morning I found Colt, my youngest, with a calculator in his hands. Of course, it was covered in baby slobber, and I noticed some buttons were missing from the calculator. I searched the floor for the missing buttons but found none. I looked at Colt with an inquisitive expression. He looked at me and smiled. I knew then why I had not yet found any evidence of those calculator buttons. I was certain I would eventually find them with the next poopy diaper I changed. Guess what? That is exactly what happened. Colt had ingested those small, rubber buttons, and the proof of what he had put in did come out. I think it took several poopy diapers before the evidence of his "meal" came to an end.

The same is true for anything we put inside of us. What do we ingest every day in our minds, bodies, and spirits? Is it beneficial, or is there evidence that it is harmful? First Corinthians 6:12 says, "All things are lawful for me, but all things are not helpful. All things are lawful for me, but I will not be brought under the power of any." There is always evidence of what we store up internally. In Matthew 12:34, Jesus gives a rebuke to those who played a good religious game but were merely "white-washed tombs" (Matthew 23:27). Evidence of their evil hearts came out in how they spoke: "You brood of vipers! How can you who are evil say anything good? For from the overflow of the heart the mouth speaks." We might think we can hide the evidence of what we put into our lives, but it won't be hidden for long. It might be subtle at first, but the more you put in, the more it builds up to produce an excretion of either good or bad. It will reveal those things for which you have an appetite, whether godly or ungodly.

If Colt had continued to eat buttons off calculators, it might have caused big problems in his digestive system. We needed to quickly correct his need to put those buttons in his mouth and change his appetite for things not beneficial to him. "I eagerly expect and hope that I will in no way be ashamed but will have sufficient courage so that now as always Christ will be exalted in my body, whether by life or by death" (Philippians 1:20). As people of God, bought with the precious atoning blood of Jesus Christ, let us put in only what can edify and strengthen what our God has given. "For you were bought at a price; therefore glorify God in your body and in your spirit, which are God's" (1 Corinthians 6:20). Feed on what is good and profitable so that others will see Jesus in you. May every part of us represent and glorify the Lord in what we put inside our hearts.

Revelation: Putting the wrong stuff in will be evident by what comes out.

FEELS SO GOOD TO LAY DOWN

WRITE DOWN WHAT THE HOLY SPIRIT SAYS TO YOU:

_____

_____

_____

_____

_____

_____

_____

_____

_____

_____

_____

_____

_____

_____

_____

_____

_____

_____

_____

_____

_____

LESSON 8

Mommy Twister

Ruth 3:1; 1 Kings 3:25–26; 2 Kings 4:30; Psalm 91:12; Psalm 131:2; Isaiah 49:15; Isaiah 66:13; Matthew 7:11; Mark 7:25–26; 1 Corinthian 13:4–7

Bold power and glorious majesty are wrapped around her as she laughs with joy over the latter days. Her teachings are filled with wisdom and kindness as loving instruction pours from her lips. She watches over the ways of her household and meets every need they have.
—**Proverbs 31:25–27** TPT

But we were gentle among you, just as a nursing mother cherishes her own children. So, affectionately longing for you, we were well pleased to impart to you not only the gospel of God, but also our own lives, because you had become dear to us.
—**1 Thessalonians 2:7–8**

A mother's love is incomparable to any other relationship on earth. I also believe that about a father's love too. Each one has unique attributes that nurture the *whole* child. Both are desperately needed. As a mother of two boys, though, I can testify to my heart and the genuine love I have for my children. I'm sure every woman reading this can certainly identify. The bond between a mother and son is really special. You carry him in your womb for nine months, singing to him and talking to him. We feed our sons. We do everything we can to make sure we do not harm them in any way. Our bodies change drastically. The extra weight and stretch marks are proof of a precious miraculous life that you've grown inside of you. It is a beautiful commitment, and it is a sacrificial commitment. The reward is tremendous!

Special needs mommies—I like to call them "extraordinary"—take that "sacrificial love" to the next level. We have literally committed our entire lives to wiping bottoms, spoon-feeding, shaving, bathing, and even communicating for our children. Twenty-four hours a day, seven days a week, we are there. If you are blessed with sympathetic family and friends, you might get a break every once in a blue moon. However, the heavy responsibility of you being the only one who can meet every need for your child is always on your mind. That is why I have to completely surrender daily to Yahweh's (YHWH's) strength and power.

My husband is a truly remarkable daddy. I have never witnessed anyone as tender, compassionate, dedicated, and committed to taking complete care of his son as does my precious husband. Even though he has deployed several times for months at time and flown missions that take him away from our family for weeks, he has always managed to make a way to be with me for every medical test and doctor's appointment for our son Clemmie.

There was one year, though, when he was stationed in Korea. The boys and I stayed in Maryland because of Clemmie's medical needs. That year, we relied on family members to help. They all took turns filling in the spaces where Daddy was missing. It was truly a loving display to me, the boys, and my husband, Shad. We had scheduled a new experimental test this same year for Clemmie. This test would require for Clemmie to be awake while the neurologist looked at his brain. This test was also to be done in Detroit, Michigan. With my helpmate stationed all the way in Korea, my father-in-law immediately volunteered to go with us in Shad's stead while MawMaw stayed with our youngest son, Colt. So, Clemmie, PawPaw, and I loaded up in our Chevy Suburban and headed north. The travel time was to be about nine hours from our house in Huntingtown, Maryland, to the hospital in Detroit, Michigan. All was going well until the eight-hour and fifty-nine-minute mark of our trip. The Sub shut down, and we literally coasted into the drop-off area of the hospital. Talk about supernatural delivery to our destination! Still more evidence of our heavenly Father's provision and protection was that my father-in-law, Bill, could fix anything. I am not exaggerating! He spent most of his adult life working on airplanes. He was the most mechanically minded man I'd ever met, besides my husband, who learned from the master. So, if I was going to break down so far away from home, Bill Vinson would be the one I would want there with me. Bill encouraged me to go ahead with Clemmie into the hospital to complete the testing. He assured me he would take care of everything else. I was confident he would.

As Clem and I made our way inside the hospital, my heart was pounding because of the unfamiliar place and the fact that I knew Clemmie would need to be awake for this particular test. Every major procedure before this had been done under sedation. Vital signs were taken, and then we were on our way to the room to be tested. As with just about every medical procedure Clem has had, the nursing staff was so gracious and kind. The nurse in charge gave instructions on where Clem was to lie down and how still he needed to be. Clemmie was around nine years old at that time, so he wasn't as small as he used to be, and the table for the exam was just big enough for him to lie on comfortably by himself. However, he needed to be in a certain position and stay that way throughout the procedure. I quickly realized that I needed to position myself partially on the table to help Clemmie feel secure in the test. I threw my right leg and right arm up on the table and held Clem close to me while my left foot was on the floor and my left arm hung freely to help balance me. I held that position for what seemed to be over an hour, and I was determined to hold it forever if it meant that Clemmie would be alright. It seemed to have really touched the nurses, because each one of them told me how beautiful and sacrificial it was for me to bear my son up like that. I was reminded of Isaiah 41:10: "Don't be afraid, for I am with you. Don't be discouraged, for I am your God. I will strengthen you and help you. I will hold you up with my victorious right hand" (NLT). At that moment, among many others, my faithful Father was upholding and strengthening me so that I could uphold Clem. Because of this moment, I can see this Scripture come to life vividly in my mind. Thank You, Lord!

Revelation: The perfect love of our heavenly Father keeps us secure, stable, and fixed. He bears us up and upholds us with His righteous right hand.

WRITE DOWN WHAT THE HOLY SPIRIT SAYS TO YOU:

LESSON 9

"Get in Here Now!"

Proverbs 14:27; Isaiah 1:19; John 14:15;
1 Peter 1:14; 1 John 5:3

I will hurry, without delay, to obey your commands.
—Psalm 119:60 NLT

"Today, if you will hear His voice, do not harden your hearts as in rebellion. . . . They shall not enter My rest."
—Hebrews 3:7–8, 11

Some of you might still be wondering what happened with my father-in-law, Bill, and the broken-down Suburban. After Clem and I left Bill with the Sub and went in for the tests, Bill called around and found a mechanic who could get our vehicle in as soon as possible. We were far away from home and very unfamiliar with Detroit. Again, I was so thankful that Bill was with us. God knew we needed him. The diagnosis for the Suburban was a bad fuel pump, so we found a hotel for the night and waited while the vehicle was being fixed. A little over twenty-four hours after we first coasted into the hospital drop-off zone, we had a working vehicle to take us back home. We were so grateful, and ready to get back to familiar territory.

The drive back home was going smoothly until we had to stop to refuel. We pulled into a gas station in Pennsylvania, and Bill began to fill up the Sub while Clemmie and I went in to find a restroom and get him a Dr Pepper. We took our time, knowing the Suburban had a big tank to fill. As Clem and I leisurely strolled out of the convenient store, I heard the screech of tires and saw the Suburban quickly approaching us, almost like Bill was trying to perform a "spin-out" move. He had the passenger window lowered, and with a look of urgency, he said, "Get in here *now*!" His cheeks were rosy-red, and his lips barely moved over his tightly clenched teeth. Again, he spoke the words, "Get in here now," just in case I had not understood the first time he said it. At this point, I knew just to do what he said to do and get in the car. I put Clem in his car seat without buckling him in, then quickly hopped in the passenger seat up front. As we took off, my mind was still begging the question, *What in the world has happened? What has my father-in-law done?* I reached behind my seat to buckle Clem in as Bill began to explain why he wanted to flee the scene so rapidly. Evidently, when the mechanics had replaced the fuel pump, they did not adequately tighten the fuel hose back in place. As Bill was filling the gas tank at the gas station, fuel began pouring out of the tank, creating a puddle of fuel on the ground. He could only imagine men in HAZMAT suits coming and keeping us there for hours. That was definitely not ideal for our situation, hence the quick escape. This experience would become something we laughed about for years.

As I replay all this in my mind, I can't help but wonder why I didn't question Bill as he issued the command to "Get in here now!" Why would I immediately do as he said without hesitation? Well, I can honestly say that it is because I knew my father-in-law. I knew that when his cheeks were red and his teeth were clenched, he meant business. I recognized the urgency in his voice, a voice I knew from past experiences. I also knew that he would only tell me to do something if it meant he was saving me from something worse. I trusted his character. I trusted his judgment. I trusted his heart for Clemmie and me. I did not need to question his motives. I was confident that he only wanted the very best for his daughter-in-law and his grandson.

Even more so is my confidence and trust in my heavenly Father. I've learned His character over the years. I've seen His love on display. I've witnessed His promises being fulfilled. I know His heart, and that the plans He has for me are plans to prosper and not to harm. They are plans to give me a hope and a future (Jeremiah 29:11). As I learn to trust Him more, I can quickly respond to His voice. The more I do that, the easier it gets to hear His direction and follow without hesitation. Psalm 119:32 says, "I will run the course of Your commandments, for You shall enlarge my heart." The Hebrew word for *run* used in this verse means "to rush" or "bring hastily toward" His commandments. There is a sense of urgency there to obey His commandments, for our good and for His glory! The faster we learn to obey, the greater the understanding of why we should obey will be. How many times do we delay our obedience for one reason or another and then wonder why there are problems in our lives? How many of our problems would not be problems at all if we simply rushed to obey our heavenly Father? What if we were to follow without question what He is telling us to do in His Word and through the Spirit's leading? Will He not "throw open the floodgates of heaven and pour out so much blessing that there will not be room enough to store it" (Malachi 3:10)? Sounds good to me!

As I fondly remember this time with my father-in-law, who went to be with Jesus in 2016, I know that if he cared for us so deeply, why would I doubt that my God cares for us any less and desires to give us the very best of gifts (Matthew 7:11)?

Revelation: Learn to obey and follow at the exact moment of the Holy Spirit's leading.

"GET IN HERE NOW!"

WRITE DOWN WHAT THE HOLY SPIRIT SAYS TO YOU:

LESSON 10

"Clem, Quit Chunkin' Your Chicken!"

Part 1

Psalm 119:18; Matthew 13:13–15; Acts 13:14, 45; Acts 17:10–12: James 1:21

Oh, taste and see that the L<small>ORD</small> is good; blessed is the man who trusts in Him!
—Psalm 34:8

I fed you with milk, not solid food; for you were not yet able to receive it. Even now you are still not ready.
—1 Corinthians 3:2 <small>AMP</small>

My boys really like Sonic. In fact, to this day, Clem loves to take a ride in "the little white car" and make the trip to Sonic. I think it's the convenience of being able to sit in "the little white car," order our food in "the little white car," and not have the pressure of someone waiting behind us in a drive-thru line—in "the little white car." When Clem was about three years old, we pulled into a Sonic in Enid, Oklahoma, where we were stationed at the time. Clem had asked for "ki-kin" and "fwy," so I proceeded to order him the Sonic popcorn chicken and fries. When we got the food, I handed him his chicken and fries, and for one reason or another, he began throwing his popcorn chicken on the car floor. Now, I was thinking, *Why in the world would you be throwing perfectly good chicken on the floor?* and *I'm going to have to clean that up!* Was the chicken bad? I sniffed. It smelled and looked fine (for Sonic, anyway). Why waste what was intended to nourish you and fill your belly? I exclaimed, "Clem, quit chunkin' your chicken!"

How often do we waste the "meat" that God has given us in His Word because we are either frivolous with it, thinking it not important enough to eat, or because we crave something different, or we're simply not ready for it. The apostle Paul experienced the refusal to receive the Word he preached by some at Philippi. However, when he arrived at the church at Thessalonica, he thanked God for them "because when you received the word of God which you heard from us, you welcomed it not as the word of men, but as it is in truth, the word of God, which also effectively works in you who believe" (1 Thessalonians 2:13). Are we ready to receive *all* the infallible, inerrant Word of God, or do we pick and choose what we want to eat of it?

"CLEM, QUIT CHUNKIN' YOUR CHICKEN!"

Hebrews 5:13 says, "For everyone who partakes only of milk is not accustomed to the word of righteousness, for he is an infant." Do we truly believe the Word of God to be effective and accomplishing what He sent it to do? (Isaiah 55:11; Psalm 107:20; Hebrews 4:12). I'm still not sure of the reason for Clemmie's open protest in eating the chicken that day, but I do know that I paid money for it. I purchased it so that he would grow and receive benefit from it. I also purchased it because he asked for it. So, why would he treat it with such disregard?

Does our heavenly Father ever wonder why we might disregard the price He paid for us, the life of His Son? He made a substantially greater purchase for us at the cross. Jesus is the "Word . . . made flesh" (see John 1:14). The Word walked among us and gave us the perfect picture of our God's will and heart for all of mankind. Jesus is our physical example of how to live. "Christ is the visible image of the invisible God" (Colossians 1:15 NLT). He is also the "Lamb of God who takes away the sins of the world!" (John 1:29), and, just as the Israelites had to eat *all* of the spotless, firstborn male lamb before they were set free from Egyptian slavery (Exodus 12:5–11), we must receive *all* of the spotless, firstborn Lamb of God in order to be *completely* set free from sin and its penalty. We must be very careful not to leave out anything, or partake of only *some* of the Lamb of God because it might seem unpalatable. Jesus' complete sacrifice and atonement at the cross may go far beyond our human understanding, but unless we "eat" of it and "drink" of it in its *entirety*, we will remain enslaved to something (John 6:53–54). "Bless the LORD, O my soul; and all that is within me, bless His holy name! Bless the LORD, O my soul, and forget not all His benefits: who forgives all your iniquities, who heals all your diseases, who redeems your life from destruction, who crowns you with lovingkindness and tender mercies, who satisfies your mouth with good things, so that your youth is renewed like the eagle's" (Psalm 103:1–5).

The *written Word* of God was given to us, inspired by the Holy Spirit, and penned by godly men, some of whom were in Jesus' inner circle of friends. Through the Holy Spirit's prompting, these men wrote about His coming; His ministry; and His death, burial, resurrection, and commission to all who believe. It has been tested and proved over thousands of years by those who claim to be believers in Jesus Christ, and even those who do not. In 1 Corinthians 3, Paul talks about wanting to give Christians in the church .at Corinth the "meat" of Scripture, but he could not. "I gave you milk, not solid food, for you were not yet ready. Indeed, even now you are not yet ready." They were not yet ready to receive the "solid food" of the Word because they had not yet matured in their faith in Jesus Christ. They could not handle the "meat." Hebrews 5:14 (NKJV) says, "But solid food belongs to those who are of full age, that is, those who by reason of use have their senses exercised to discern both good and evil." Once you taste solid food, you never want to return to the milk. Your taste buds will crave that solid food, and milk alone will not satisfy your craving. In fact, you will reject anything that is not "solid." We mommies understand that in helping our babies graduate off the milk onto eating solids, we are helping them to grow (1 Peter 2:2) and not stay as an infant. Now, maybe Clem was chunkin' that chicken because he discerned that it was not beneficial, being that it was fast food. That is entirely possible. However, many times we waste the precious "meat" or "solid food" because we don't see its value. We don't truly understand the price that was paid for us to have it and receive all its benefits. His words really are "life to those who find them, and health to all their flesh" (Proverbs 4:22). May we never reject them but receive and live. Just "taste and see" (Psalm 34:8)!

Revelation: Stop wasting the "meat" that you should be eating. Be ready to receive what is solid food for the soul before you toss what is beneficial away.

WRITE DOWN WHAT THE HOLY SPIRIT SAYS TO YOU:

LESSON 11

"Clem, Quit Chunkin' Your Chicken!"

Part 2

Jeremiah 2:8; Jeremiah 10:21; Jeremiah 23:1–2;
Jeremiah 12:10; Ezekiel 34:9; Hebrews 13:7, 17;
James 1:21–22; 1 Timothy 3

> *"And I will give you shepherds according to My heart, who will feed you with knowledge and understanding."*
> **—Jeremiah 3:15**

. . . to be compassionate shepherds who tenderly care for God's flock and who feed them well, for you have the responsibility to guide, protect, and oversee. Consider it a joyous pleasure and not merely a religious duty. Lead from the heart under God's leadership—not as a way to gain finances

> *dishonestly but as a way to eagerly and cheerfully serve. Don't be controlling tyrants but lead others by your beautiful examples to the flock.*
> —**1 Peter 5:2–3** TPT

This lesson was initially meant to be about Pharisees who misused and abused the "solid food" of Scripture as "stones" to throw at those whom they were to "shepherd" and "feed" "with knowledge and understanding." The purpose of the shepherd was to show the people the heart of God. The Pharisees fell far short of that. Instead, they used the food to hurt the people, and they wondered why they found them malnourished. If we are not careful, we can become—and many of us have become—the same tool used to wound the brokenhearted instead of leading them to the Healer. I know there have been times when I have used "the chicken" to "chunk" at folks without the direct guidance of the Holy Spirit. That can be so destructive and harmful for the cause of Christ. May true compassion for the lost and hurting be our motivation to lead them to Jesus in order to be reconciled to God the Father under the direction of the Holy Spirit.

The more I prayed about this second part of the "chunkin' your chicken" lesson, I believe the Lord gave me compassion specifically for the shepherds and overseers of our congregations. As the daughter, and the granddaughter, of pastors, I understand the demands. I've seen the tremendous pull and outpouring required to serve the people. I've witnessed the good, the bad, and the ugly business of church. It is no surprise to me why so many of "the called" fall into the bondage of sin themselves, or simply tire of all the expectations and eventually throw up their hands in defeat. It breaks my heart, and I'm sure it grieves our Lord. The people of God must understand that their pastor is not to be their spoon-feeder. As an overseer, the pastor oversees the church, making sure it is adequately equipped, or at least steadfast in its pursuit to be equipped, to minister to others themselves. A pastor is not the answer to your problems—Jesus is, and until we get this right, our pastors will continue to burn out. I believe we've forgotten what James 5:13 says: "Are there any believers in your fellowship suffering great hardship and distress? Encourage them to pray!" It does not say, "Encourage them to tell all their woes to the pastor." We have become too dependent on our leaders to feed us instead of learning self-care in our personal relationship with God the Father, Son, and Holy Spirit. Go to the Good Shepherd to get fed, not the under-shepherd.

I also know from experience that the reason so many pastors have devastating results in their ministry is for one main reason. This is not a condemnation against these pastors, but hopefully, it is a "spurring on" to continue the race with endurance. While they are busy scripting their next sermon and ministering to the flock, and while many can quote a Scripture for every kind of issue, the problem is the lack of ingesting the food for themselves. A pastor must themselves prepare the food, receive the food for themselves, put it in, chew on it, swallow, and then digest it for the people. There needs to be an understanding that the people will become malnourished if they do not take time to partake of the "Bread of Life" and the "Living Water" for themselves (John 4:10; 6:35). Are they going back to the "milk," or is their appetite increasing for "solid food"? Scripture issues a powerful warning about shepherds who do more harm than good for God's people. Jeremiah 10:21 says, "For the shepherds have become dull-hearted, and have not sought the LORD; therefore they shall not prosper, and all their flocks shall be scattered." How do we not become "dull-hearted," or "stupid," as the Tree of Life version states? We fellowship with the Savior and eat!

We must understand that all of us, when not feeding on the Word for ourselves, will fall short. Pastors and church leaders are no different. Those who are not pastors need to be able to recognize if their pastor needs time to replenish. Several times in my life and ministry I have given the food to so many people, and yet I have forgotten to feed on the Word through my own independent study and quiet time with Jesus. We must encourage each other not to forsake the meal with the Master. Humility is key, and pride in one's title and status must be repented of. This applies to all the "equippers" (Ephesians 4:11–12) of the saints: apostles, prophets, evangelists, pastors, and teachers. If any of us holds these positions of authority in the body of Christ, we need to consistently be feeding on the solid Word of God. Though compassionately tossing that "chicken" with the intent to help others know the Savior is noble, why not instead do as Jesus did and invite them to sit and enjoy the feast that you are also enjoying? I'm reminded of something my PawPaw would say as we ate together: "Butter 'em, and pass 'em while they're hot!"

As we sit together, supping with the Savior, let us pass the food with a passion and motivation to be nourished by the "living and powerful" (Hebrews 4:12) Word of God. As a result, we will all grow into maturity for His honor and glory.

Revelation: None of us is beyond needing nourishment through the "meat" of the Word of God. Be still, and enjoy the food and fellowship at the Master's table.

WRITE DOWN WHAT THE HOLY SPIRIT SAYS TO YOU:

_____

_____

_____

_____

_____

_____

_____

_____

_____

_____

_____

_____

_____

_____

_____

_____

_____

_____

_____

_____

LESSON 12

"Slow Down, Mommy! I'm Spilling My Chocolate Milk!"

Psalm 46:10; Proverbs 21:5; Isaiah 40:31;
Ecclesiastes 3:1; Matthew 11:28–30 Ephesians 5:16;
Philippians 4:6–7; 2 Peter 3:8–9;
Hebrews 12:1; James 5:7

Zeal without knowledge is not good, or to act hastily and miss the way.
—**Proverbs 19:2** TLV

There remains therefore a rest for the people of God. For he who has entered His rest has himself also ceased from his works as God did from His. Let us therefore be diligent to enter that rest, lest anyone fall according to the same example of disobedience.
—**Hebrews 4:9–11**

Another trip to Sonic. Another lesson learned. This time the teacher was Colt, my youngest. He used to love ordering chocolate milk with his meal. Now, at fourteen years old, it is Powerade, but at three years old, it was Sonic's chocolate milk. For one reason or another, that day, instead of eating our lunch there at the stall, we need to get somewhere—fast! I believe I've learned better time management since then, but on that particular day, at that particular time, I was in a rush. As I put the car in Reverse to back out of the Sonic stall, then put it in Drive to leave, it must have felt like we were in a getaway car for an illegal bank robbery. Colt was not all that impressed with my driving skills. The quick turns and bumps in the road caused his milk to spill. He was never at a loss for words, but this emphatic statement got my attention: "Slow down, Mommy! I'm spilling my chocolate milk!" I apologized with a giggle and slowed my roll.

I love how lessons often come through our children. We must be wise enough to listen. We must acknowledge that the devil wants to keep us busy. The enemy wants us in a rush. He is the author of confusion and chaos, and if he can get us frazzled and hurried in life, we won't live in the perfect peace God has authored for us (1 Corinthians 14:33). Satan wants to steal our joy, kill us, and destroy everything good that God created. If we do not slow down and appreciate every one of the moments we've been given, he has, at least, worn us out enough to lessen the effectiveness of our calling and ministries.

It is so easy to get in a rush with life. The expectations we put on ourselves, and the fact that time does not stand still, creates a whirlwind of busyness leading to missed opportunities and blindness to all the little blessings the Lord gives. We can overlook those blessings in the pursuit of accomplishing tasks that we deem worthy. Children are blessings. Psalm 127:3 (NLT) says that "children are a gift from the LORD; they are a reward from him." It is because of my children that I am able to understand more fully the love my heavenly Father has for me. It is also because of my children that I experience many of these teachable moments I write about. Praise God from whom all blessings flow, and take time to be still (Psalm 46:10) with the Lord God and with those you love. Be intentionally present. Show your children what it means to serve Jehovah Shalom. "Now may the Lord of peace Himself give you peace always in every way. The Lord be with you all" (2 Thessalonians 3:16).

Revelation: Slow down! Take time to enjoy every moment God gives you. Rest and be thankful.

FEELS SO GOOD TO LAY DOWN

WRITE DOWN WHAT THE HOLY SPIRIT SAYS TO YOU:

_____

_____

_____

_____

_____

_____

_____

_____

_____

_____

_____

_____

_____

_____

_____

_____

_____

_____

_____

_____

LESSON 13

Wearing Daddy's Shoes

Proverbs 4:1–13; Proverbs 8:4-22; Proverbs 13:1; Proverbs 15:20; Proverbs 19:20; Ecclesiastes 4:13; Isaiah 30:1; Isaiah 40:31; 1 Corinthians 11:1; Philippians 3:17; 2 Timothy 3:15–17; James 1:3–5; James 5:7–8; 1 Peter 5:5–7

Rejoice, O young man, in your youth, and let your heart cheer you in the days of your youth; walk in the ways of your heart, and in the sight of your eyes; but know that for all these God will bring you into judgement.
—**Ecclesiastes 11:9**

The proverbs of Solomon the son of David, king of Israel: To know wisdom and instruction . . . justice, judgment, and equity; to give prudence to the simple, to the young man knowledge and discretion—a wise man will hear and increase learning, and a man of understanding will attain wise counsel.
—**Proverbs 1:1–5**

> *Therefore, laying aside all malice, all deceit, hypocrisy, envy, and all evil speaking, as newborn babes, desire the pure milk of the word, that you may grow thereby, if indeed you have tasted that the Lord is gracious.*
> **—1 Peter 2:1–3**

How many of us as little children liked to pretend to be grown-ups by wearing our parents' clothes and shoes? Little girls like to put on their mommy's makeup and high heels, and little boys like to wear their daddy's shirt and tie. It is so sweet to see a child imitate and emulate their parents. It is also sobering to see how much our children watch what we do, listen to what we say, and imitate us. Our *actions* and our *words* are very important in how we "train up a child in the way he should go" (Proverbs 22:6). Both are very instrumental in either leading them *to* Jesus or away *from* Him. We must be vigilant in our pursuit of His holiness so that our children will receive the benefits of a godly inheritance.

I remember our youngest, Colt, missing his daddy when he was deployed. The first thing he wanted to do was walk around the house wearing his daddy's shoes. He played with his toys in daddy's big shoes. I could hear Colt coming before I saw him because those shoes were so much bigger than his little feet, and Colt worked hard to keep them on with every step. At times, Colt would trip, sometimes falling. One shoe might even come off, but Colt was persistent to keep both shoes on to walk like Daddy and talk like Daddy. He loved his daddy so much, and he wanted to be just like him. He still does.

There is something precious about loving your daddy so much that you think you can and should fill his shoes, especially in his absence. We find ourselves still wanting to fill those shoes as we grow. Of course, now I'm talking more figuratively. I have heard story after story of grown children who never quite felt adequate enough to fill their daddies' shoes. Some felt like complete failures and disappointments by not filling their daddies' shoes. Their comparisons and striving to be exactly like Daddy somehow always ended in failure, and that perceived failure steered the course of their lives. The constant need to prove their worth has led them into deep insecurity. That is always the end result when we try to be someone we were not created to be.

We would all do well to remember that our God made each one of us uniquely special to fulfill His purpose. Psalm 139:13–14 says, "For You formed my inward parts; You covered me in my mother's womb. I will praise You, for I am fearfully and wonderfully made; marvelous are Your works, and that my soul knows very well." When our soul truly knows that we were not created to fill anyone else's shoes, we can enjoy the growing. When we are confident of who we are in Christ, it leaves little room for insecurities. When we are confident in the promises of His Word, we can live free of comparisons. In fact, when we understand that almighty God created us to glorify Him in life, and not meet the standards of others, we take our eyes off others and put our focus on fulfilling the purpose for which we were created. When we remain humble and teachable to learn from godly elders, we can effectively grow into that purpose. Unfortunately, many of us try to put on the big clothes before we are ready. We have not taken the time to be an understudy of the wise, and we become haughty, yet still insecure, in our own abilities. This is when we trip and fall.

It is okay not to have it all figured out. It is okay not to be perfect, trusting that you are being *perfected* by the One who *is* perfect. The Lord knows you too well to think you can do anything without His hands and feet guiding. It is good to be like a child and sit at your Abba's feet listening and learning. It is good to imitate your Father. It is good to imitate earthly spiritual fathers and mothers. Paul told the church at Corinth to "imitate me" (1 Corinthians 4:16). Hebrews 13:7 says, "Remember your leaders, who spoke the word of God to you. Consider the outcome of their way of life and imitate their faith" (TLV). Let your heavenly Father do His work and make your feet bigger to walk in His "shoes." "Be imitators of God in everything you do, for then you will represent your Father as his beloved sons and daughters" (Ephesians 5:1 TPT). Get to know Him. Grow into someone who is not only His child but, through maturity in faith, His friend (John 15:14–15).

I've known too many people who've undoubtedly had powerful conversion experiences, finding themselves deep in the grips of what they were pulled from simply because they did not give the time necessary to be taught how to walk in His ways. They were so overcome with the emotion and excitement of being set free that nothing was going to stop them from ministering. Church leaders, seeing that excitement, immediately throw them into the deep end of the pool in church ministry, and before too long, these new converts were leading on the praise team or given leadership over the prayer ministry. Too much too fast can potentially lead to pride and then destruction. We must be discipled and be patient during time of instruction.

Find spiritual fathers and mothers who are living out a proven godly life. Ask questions, take notes, and learn. We have plenty of examples of that in Scripture. Give God your heart, your time, and your ear to listen to godly instruction, whether it be through His voice, through His Word, or through others. Don't become so busy pouring out in ministry that you become malnourished and weak yourself. In His time, the shoes always fit for you to walk in perfect step with Him. "Let perseverance finish its work so that you may be mature and complete, not lacking anything" (James 1:4 NIV).

Revelation: Grow, but don't rush things. You might trip and fall if you think yourself big enough before you are ready!

WRITE DOWN WHAT THE HOLY SPIRIT SAYS TO YOU:

_____

_____

_____

_____

_____

_____

_____

_____

_____

_____

_____

_____

_____

_____

_____

_____

_____

_____

_____

_____

LESSON 14

"Are We There Yet?"

Psalm 27:13–14; Psalm 130:5; Proverbs 14:29; Micah 7:7; Hosea 12:6; Habakkuk 2:3; Galatians 5:22–23; Ephesians 4:2; Hebrews 10:36; James 5:7–8

But those who wait on the Lord shall renew their strength; they shall mount up with wings like eagles, they shall run and not be weary, they shall walk and not faint.
—Isaiah 40:31

But if we hope for what we do not yet have, we wait for it patiently.
—Romans 8:25

If you've ever taken a long road trip with your kids, you are most likely familiar with the question, "Are we there yet?" This interrogation seems to continue the whole trip until we finally lose our cool and respond, "We'll get there when we get there!" This makes the trip especially frustrating when you have a child who is not yet able to communicate verbally his wants and needs. In the heat of battle, the thought of never doing this again crosses your mind, but you will do it again . . . and again . . . and again.

Children have a limited understanding of time and distance. Young minds and emotions only understand instant gratification. If their needs and wants are not met quickly, they will cry and fuss until they get what they want. The idea of waiting for something is foreign to a child, and only if waiting is incorporated into their instruction and training will a child learn to be patient. If we always give in to their need for something to be done "right now," they will not learn how to wait. If we appease them with what they want all the time, they will grow into adults who desire instant gratification. Is this not the culture in which we live as well? I'm reminded of the song Veruca sings in the movie *Willy Wonka and the Chocolate Factory*: "I want the world. I want the whole world. I want to wrap it all up in my pocket and give it a locket. Give it to me . . . now!" Her daddy spends his days giving her all she wants when she wants it, but it never fully satisfies her.

Unlike Veruca's dad, our perfect heavenly Father knows how detrimental it is to give us what we want exactly when we want it. It's not that He does not want to give us the desires of our heart. No! It's the very opposite! "Delight yourself also in the LORD, and He shall give you the desires of your heart" (Psalm 37:4). He simply wants us to look to Him first, being satisfied in His presence, aligning our heart with His. I truly believe our heavenly Father loves the waiting. He knows full well how much the waiting benefits us. Ecclesiastes 3:1 says, "There is an appointed time for everything. And there is a time for every event under heaven." Of course, in the beginning, we might cry and throw a fit when we don't get what we want at the exact moment we ask for it. We do not understand time and distance the way our God understands time and distance. Second Peter 3:8 reveals our limited understanding of time: "But don't forget this one thing, loved ones, that with the Lord one day is like a thousand years, and a thousand years are like one day" (TLV). God sees the bigger picture, and He knows the bigger plan.

We often want to reach the destination without taking the journey. It's in the journey where we learn to be patient. "But let patience have its perfect work, that you may be perfect and complete, lacking nothing" (James 1:4). If we learn to be joyful in the journey, and even stop to smell the flowers, the destination becomes so much more meaningful and exciting. It is then that the "abundant life" Jesus paid for will unfold, and the trip will be worth the wait.

Revelation: Our God does His most powerful work in the waiting. Wait patiently and see His wondrous works unfold!

WRITE DOWN WHAT THE HOLY SPIRIT SAYS TO YOU:

LESSON 15

"Mommy, Can I Get a Puppy?"

Joshua 21:45; Psalm 27:4; Psalm 37:5;
Luke 12:48; Luke 14:28

*Take delight in the L*ORD*, and he will give you the desires of your heart.*
—**Psalm 37:4** NIV

"The one who faithfully manages the little he has been given will be promoted and trusted with greater responsibilities. But those who cheat with the little they have been given will not be considered trustworthy to receive more."
—**Luke 16:10** TPT

"Mommy, can I get a puppy?" I'm sure every parent has been asked this very question at one time or another. It's a wonderful idea to have a puppy. I mean, just think about it. Having a cute little playful ball of fur who loves you and your kids unconditionally would be great, right? Right! However, my thoughts quickly go to who will be taking care of this sweet little bundle of energy. Will it be my kids, who simply cannot live without this little puppy, or will it be the parents, who already have enough to manage and take care of? Most of us know the answer to that question. The question then begs to be asked: "Will you take care of this little puppy?" "Yes, Mommy!" I now have to make a decision based on what I believe is best for my son. I do not ignore him. I do not remain silent. There is always an answer, but this is when I have to discern *which* answer to give him: *yes*, *no*, or *wait*.

I've heard people say there have been times they've asked God for something and He has not answered. I've always had a hard time with this. Why would a loving heavenly Father *not* answer His children? "If you then, being evil, know how to give good gifts to your children, how much more will your Father who is in heaven give good things to those who ask Him!" (Matthew 7:11). I truly believe He *does* answer His children, always. Jeremiah 33:3 says, "Call to Me, and I will answer you—I will tell you great and hidden things, which you do not know" (TLV).

When God seems silent, I ask myself these questions: First, am I close enough to hear His voice? "If you abide in Me, and My words abide in you, you will ask what you desire, and it shall be done for you" (John 15:7). The Lord promises good to those who abide in His presence and dwell with Him continuously. Psalm 91 begins with

"He who dwells in the secret place of the Most High, shall abide under the shadow of the Almighty. I will say of the LORD, 'He is my refuge and my fortress; my God, in Him I will trust,'" We must dwell with Him and abide under the shadow of His wings in order to receive the benefits of His blessings. When we can honestly say, "Here's the one thing I crave from YAHWEH, the one thing I seek above all else: I want to live with him every moment in his house, beholding the marvelous beauty of YAHWEH, filled with awe, delighting in his glory and grace. I want to contemplate in his temple" (Psalm 27:4 TPT), *then* we might be close enough to Him to hear His voice when He answers. "My sheep hear My voice, and I know them, and they follow Me" (John 10:27). Are we abiding so close to Him that we can hear His voice clearly and even feel His heartbeat (John 13:23)?

Second, are voices of doubt louder than the Voice of Truth? In Job 30:20, Job exclaims, "I cry to you for help and you do not answer me; I stand, and you only look at me" (ESV). Job, though he never cursed God, still had friends who were voices of doubt and discouragement during his times of trouble. We know it was Satan who was his accuser, who asked permission to steal, kill, and destroy everything Job had. At times, it was easier for Job to feel alone in his sorrows and wonder why God was silent, but that wasn't the end of his story. God stood ready to give it all back and so much more. Is our God's voice drowned out by voices of doubt and discouragement in our life?

Finally, is the silence we perceive really a time of waiting on Him to fulfill a greater purpose? Has He already answered me with "wait"? He knows best what I need and when I need it. An answer of "wait" usually means I need time to prepare, time to grow, or time to finish something else. "Wait" usually means the time is not yet right for me to have that for which I've asked. It doesn't mean that He won't eventually give it to me, but there must be something to be learned in the process of waiting. "Wait on the LORD; be of good courage, and He shall strengthen your heart; wait, I say, on the LORD!" (Psalm 27:14). There is a refining that takes place in the waiting. It strengthens us. It teaches us. It matures us. As a parent, is this not what we want for our own children? Why would our faithful heavenly Father want to give us something without first teaching us, refining us, strengthening us, and maturing us to be the very best steward of the gift He is giving? This is true everlasting love. It is a love that cares deeply.

If I were to have answered Colt with a "yes," he would have assumed we were bringing home a puppy immediately. As a child, he did not fully understand all the preparation that needed to happen before we could get a puppy. A child's mind only sees the good in having a puppy. He thinks, *Puppy Dog Pals*. He is not thinking of what the puppy will eat and how much the puppy will eat. He has no concept of what will need to happen after the puppy eats, and how many times he will need to do that. Who is going to let him out at 2 a.m. when he needs to go potty, if he has not already gone in the house? Who will clean that up? What about the veterinary bills when he needs his shots or gets sick? Who will be training this little puppy? Will Colt teach him to sit, stay, and not chew on everything he sees? This is only the puppy stage. A puppy eventually becomes a full-grown dog that could very well live through Colt's high school and college years. Raising a puppy is a long-term commitment and responsibility. Is Colt ready for that responsibility? Am I ready to help teach Colt these responsibilities? These are all considerations I must make when responding to my then-eight-year-old son.

Would it not be more beneficial for Colt if I answered with "no" or "wait"? Each of these answers might elicit dramatically different reactions from my young son. However, evidence of his maturity, his understanding of the responsibilities involved, and the amount of trust he has in Mom and Dad will show in how he responds. If he responds by throwing a fit, is he ready? If he responds with pouting, is he ready? I would contend that both of these responses are proof that he is not yet ready. If nothing else, it proves his lack of trust and contentment in what Mom and Dad think is best, not only for him but for the whole family. I have witnessed grown adults, who claim to be mature in Christ, throw temper-tantrums when they don't get their way. I believe that is evidence of a lack of maturity in their walk with Christ. I love how James tells of the benefits of waiting: "Dear brothers and sisters, when troubles of any kind come your way, consider it an opportunity for great joy. For you know that when your faith is tested, your endurance has a chance to grow. So let it grow, for when your endurance is fully developed, you will be perfect and complete, needing nothing. If you need wisdom, ask our generous God, and he will give it to you. He will not rebuke you for asking. But when you ask him, be sure that your faith is in God alone. Do not waver, for a person with divided loyalty is as unsettled as a wave of the sea that is blown and tossed by the wind. Such people should not expect to receive anything from the Lord. Their loyalty is divided between God and the world, and they are unstable in everything they do" (James 1:2–8 NLT). Wow!

Now, I know it is not wisdom that Colt was asking for, but I pray that Colt and Clem have learned by now to trust Mom and Dad to give them what they need when they need it. We truly want them to ask us in full confidence that we will always do what is best for them, but I pray they will have the wisdom to know what is best, too. I also pray they will always respond with grace and patience, no matter the answer. When we ask something of our heavenly Father, may we ask with confidence, knowing that He will give us what is best when we are ready to receive it. May we have wisdom in the asking.

Revelation: To whom much is given, much is required. Are we ready for that responsibility? When God answers with "wait," will we wait on His will patiently and expectant of His very best gift for us?

WRITE DOWN WHAT THE HOLY SPIRIT SAYS TO YOU:

_____

_____

_____

_____

_____

_____

_____

_____

_____

_____

_____

_____

_____

_____

_____

_____

_____

_____

_____

_____

LESSON 16

A Tree Planted by Streams of Water

(Clemmie's Plant)

Jeremiah 17:8; Hosea 10:12; Malachi 4:2;
Luke 6:38; 2 Corinthians 9:6

*Blessed is the man who walks not in the counsel of
the ungodly, nor stands in the path of sinners, nor
sits in the seat of the scornful; but his delight is in
the law of the LORD, and in His law he meditates day
and night. He shall be like a tree planted by rivers
of water, that brings forth its fruit in its season,
whose leaf also shall not wither; and whatever he
does shall prosper.*
—**Psalm 1:1–3**

*Beloved, I wish above all things that you may prosper
and be in good health just as your soul prospers.*
—**3 John 2**

I must confess that it has taken me over forty years to develop somewhat of a green thumb, at least enough to help a plant thrive and grow. I have had to learn a lot. How much water is too much or not enough? How much sunlight is too much or not enough? What plants grow best in Oklahoma, California, and Maryland? And, now, what plants can survive the Texas heat? I guess I'm in a season now when I can truly pay attention to all the specific needs of each plant, but it has taken years of watching them wither away under my "care."

I'll never forget a meeting we had with our oldest son's kindergarten teacher. As we entered the classroom, we noticed small plastic cups of soil. Some of the cups were showing signs of a few small green sprouts. Some were not. As we scanned the room, our eyes were drawn to one cup where the plant was significantly fuller and greener than all the other cups. It looked as if it had had several more weeks of nourishment compared to the others. Mrs. Cain, noticing our interest in that plant, began to tell us that the vibrant plant had come from the seed planted by our son Clemmie. She explained how, while the other students had simply dropped the seeds into the soil, Clemmie took time to rub the seeds in between his fingers. He massaged the seeds into the soil. He was not distracted by what others were doing. He was fully focused on the seeds he was given. He was not hasty with the seeds, but he studied the seeds and allowed his senses to examine the little seeds. All the plants were placed into the very same environment to grow.

They were all given the same amount of water, nutrients, and sunlight, but Clem's plant was dramatically different. Clemmie had tenderly cared for his seeds from the very beginning, and his plant grew abundantly more healthy and vibrant, and in a shorter amount of time. His plant truly prospered!

Can you imagine what our lives would be like if we took the time not just to plant the seeds of truth, but to meditate and chew on them? To break them down precept upon precept and let them take root firmly in us from the very start? If we were to allow our senses to examine every word carefully, without haste, I believe God's Word would come alive in us. "This Book of the Law shall not depart from your mouth, but you shall meditate on it day and night, that you may observe to do according to all that is written in it. For then you will make your way prosperous, and then you will have good success" (Joshua 1:8). The implanted Word would become so much more alive in the light of the "Sun of Righteousness" and watered by the "Living Water" (James 1:21; Malachi 4:2; John 4:10, 14). It would grow and flourish in us beyond what we could possibly imagine, and there would be nothing our God could not accomplish in us. The world would certainly take notice and want to know our Gardener.

Revelation: Take time to meditate on God's Word day and night. Chew on it. Absorb the truth, and let it transform you into that "tree planted by streams of water."

A TREE PLANTED BY STREAMS OF WATER

WRITE DOWN WHAT THE HOLY SPIRIT SAYS TO YOU:

LESSON 17

So Close, Yet So Far Away

Psalm 16:11; Psalm 23:4; Psalm 91; Isaiah 26:3; Matthew 28:20; Romans 8:38–39

"Stay here with me, and don't be afraid. I will protect you with my own life, for the same person wants to kill us both."
—1 Samuel 22:23 NLT

"Are you weary, carrying a heavy burden? Come to me. I will refresh your life, for I am your oasis."
—Matthew 11:28 TPT

Have you ever sat in the same room with your child and still not been able to catch them when they fell or save them from something that caused them pain? I've had that feeling: *If he'd only been closer to me, I would have been able to protect him.* That has happened to me numerous times, especially with Clemmie. One time in particular,

Clem and I had awakened around our usual time: 6 a.m. Clem stood in his normal place at our kitchen island, looking at the videos on his electronic device. I had just finished pouring the water into our coffeemaker to start the coffee brewing. I went to sit down on my recliner about twelve feet from where Clemmie stood, and the next thing I heard was the cup of water Clem had on the island hitting the floor. At the same time, I heard Clemmie murmur, and as I looked over to see what was happening, I could see him go rigid and begin to fall. I jumped up, trying to run and catch him, but it was too late. Clem was on the floor, having a grand-mal seizure. I got down on the floor and held him in order to keep his head from banging against the floor again. As I held him, I prayed, declaring Isaiah 53: "By Jesus' stripes, you are healed, Clem!" I yelled for Shad, who was in our bedroom. Any other Wednesday, Shad would have been on a four-day trip away from home, but this particular Wednesday, he was at home on vacation. My yelling also awakened Colt. They both ran into the kitchen and jumped into action. After providing my initial jolt into action to keep my son physically protected, the Holy Spirit brought to my mind His Word, which says that I have "authority to trample upon serpents and scorpions, and over all the power of the enemy, nothing shall by any means hurt you" (Luke 10:19), and so I took hold of that authority! *I bind you, seizing spirit, and demand you, in the name of Jesus, to leave Clemmie alone!* Clem's body immediately began to relax. I can testify to this happening each time I have taken that authority. I pray that you never find that to be insensitive or take offense to my scriptural stance, but it is very clear in Scripture that seizures are caused by unclean spirits. Look at Matthew 17:14–18; Mark 9:17–27; and Luke 9:37–43, regarding the boy who suffered with seizures. Mark's account in Mark 9:17 calls it a "mute spirit." Matthew and Luke also refer to it as a spirit. "Jesus rebuked the demon, and it came out of him; and the child was cured from that very hour" (Matthew 17:18). Jesus says in Matthew 16:19, "And I will give you the keys of the kingdom of heaven, and whatever you bind on earth will be bound in heaven, and whatever you loose on earth will be loosed in heaven." I believe it!

If we truly believe the Word of God, then we must believe that "we do not wrestle against flesh and blood, but against principalities, against powers, against the rulers of the darkness of this age, against spiritual hosts of wickedness in the heavenly places" (Ephesians 6:12). I can truthfully testify that by taking authority over these unclean spirits through the life-giving power of the Holy Spirit, I have seen them flee and leave my son alone. I boldly stand on His promises. If you have received the Holy Spirit, you have that same authority as well. In fact, Mark's account of the Commission Jesus gave to those who believe is this: "And these signs shall follow those who believe: In My name they will cast out demons; they will speak with new tongues; they will take up serpents; and if they drink anything deadly, it will by no means hurt them; they will lay hands on the sick, and they will recover" (Mark 16:17–

18). If I am to "go into all the world and preach the gospel to every creature," then I need to believe I will be able to do exactly what Jesus tells me I will be able to do—and it starts in my own home.

Clemmie had a big bump on his head from the fall that day, but the bump was nearly unnoticeable the next day. After an event like this, Clemmie always leans in a little closer to me, as if he understands the importance of keeping Mommy and Daddy close for safety. Shad and I usually watch him intently and stay closer to him, too. As Clemmie's mother, who loves him deeply, I never want to be too far away so I can keep him from harm. We are definitely reminded to stay vigilant against the evil schemes of the wicked one, whose only goal is to "steal, kill, and destroy" (John 10:10). When things are going well, we are in danger of becoming complacent and comfortable in our everyday lives, and that is how Satan wants us to be. Most families do not have special needs kids in the home, so they are not fully aware that the battle for their children's souls still rages. I am grateful for the constant reminder to put on the spiritual armor. We must "stay alert! Watch out! Your adversary the devil prowls around like a roaring lion, searching for someone to devour" (1 Peter 5:8 TLV). Satan's schemes may be a little more subtle in your life, but believe me, if you are a child of the King of kings, the devil will be after you. Take authority!

Although we truly believe that Clemmie has been healed by Jesus' stripes (Isaiah 53:5; 1 Peter 2:24), the battle over his life continues. Our God is not done yet, and we choose to take Him at His Word—for however long it takes. We all need these reminders to stay close to the "Mighty Warrior who saves" (Zephaniah 3:17 NIV). I love how our God not only saves, but He takes "delight in [us] with gladness. With his love, he will calm all [our] fears. He will rejoice over [us] with joyful songs" (NLT). The thought of my heavenly Father singing over Clemmie makes my heart happy. Unlike us, our heavenly Father is never distracted, and He is never too busy to protect and deliver us from all harm. Psalm 91 says, "Whoever dwells (abides) in the shelter of the Most High will rest in the shadow of the Almighty" (verse 10). We must stay close to our God and abide in His presence continuously. Under His wings is where we truly find refuge and safety. In fact, Psalm 91 promises that if we dwell in the secret place of the Most High, no evil will overtake us, and no plague will come near us. This reminds me to never leave my Father's side; although we're never too far out of His reach, we can still wander just far enough to get hit by the fiery darts of the wicked one. Come in close, dear ones, and let Him protect and save.

Revelation: The more we press into the Father, the safer we become. Remain with Him.

WRITE DOWN WHAT THE HOLY SPIRIT SAYS TO YOU:

LESSON 18

"Mom, You're Beautiful"

1 Chronicles 16:29; Psalm 29:2; Psalm 90:17; Psalm 96:9;
Proverbs 23:24; Isaiah 61:10

Her sons and her daughters arise in one accord to extol her virtues, and her husband arises to speak of her in glowing terms.
—**Proverbs 31:28** TPT

"Nevertheless I have this against you, that you have left your first love."
—**Revelation 2:4**

At four years old, Colt looked at me with sincerity in his eyes and said, "Mom, you're beautiful." Now, at fourteen, Colt, though still thoughtful and loving when we're at home, is far more concerned with the dudes around him and how they might make fun of him if he were to make over his momma. I have to admit that has bothered me a little, but Shad has reminded me that it is part of a young man's growing up into independence. I want Colt to become independent and responsible. And while I don't necessarily want him to need me, I do miss those moments of affection that show me how much he loves me.

I can't help but wonder if our heavenly Father feels grieved in our own spiritual "teenage" years. Somewhere in the middle of our growing relationship with Him, we often lose sight of wanting to just look at Him with sincerity in our hearts and say, "Oh, Lord, You're beautiful" (Psalm 27:4). Somewhere between the milk and the meat, we don't have time to sit at His feet and behold Him. We find ourselves busy trying to understand Him with the carnal mind but detaching the heart. We are more concerned about what others think and less concerned about His heart.

In the book of Revelation, John writes a letter to the church of Ephesus, warning them of losing sight of their first love.

> *"I know your works, your labor, your patience, and that you cannot bear those who are evil. And you have tested those who say they are apostles and are not, and have found them liars; and you have persevered and have patience, and have labored for My name's sake and have not become weary. Nevertheless, I have this against you, that you have left your first love."*
>
> **—Revelation 2:2–4**

"MOM, YOU'RE BEAUTIFUL"

If this church had been measured strictly according to the Law, they would have received an A+. They were following the rule book, but God was not pleased. They had forgotten Him. They were so focused on the commands that they neglected abiding in the presence of the One whose commands they were following. I believe this is where many in the Church are today. We are all so involved in church activities that we never stop to simply behold our Savior, and, like Mary, sit at His feet in awe of Him (Luke 10:38–42).

We should find *pleasure* in His presence. Abiding with Him should be a *valuable thing* and the *desire* of every born-again believer. When we *desire*, find *pleasure* in, and see Him as *valuable*, we experience what the psalmist meant in Psalm 1:2: "But his *delight* is in the law of the Lord, and in His law he meditates day and night." The more we *delight* in the Lord and His Word, the closer to Him we become. When we truly experience His beautiful presence, we are more likely to remain there, where we find "fullness of joy" and "pleasures forevermore" (Psalm 16:11).

I don't know if my youngest son will ever say those words again to me, and I'm sure he'll change his mind about wanting to live with his dad and me forever. That's okay. One day he will have a wife and a home of his own, where he will *delight* in the Lord, and that is good. Above all, my prayer is for him to never forget to "dwell in the secret place of the Most High" (Psalm 91:1) and delight in the presence of his Savior. May these words forever be on his lips: "Oh, Lord, You're beautiful," and may he mean it with all his heart. "Here's the one thing I crave from YAHWEH, the one thing I seek above all else: I want to live with him every moment in his house, beholding the marvelous beauty of YAHWEH, filled with awe, delighting in his glory and grace. I want to contemplate in his temple" (Psalm 27:4 TPT). Amen.

Revelation: What matters most to our God is the time we spend abiding with Him. He loves to be close to us. Behold Him and dwell in the beauty of His holiness. Return to your first love.

"MOM, YOU'RE BEAUTIFUL"

WRITE DOWN WHAT THE HOLY SPIRIT SAYS TO YOU:

LESSON 19

My Ghost Story

1 Samuel 12:24; Psalm 91; Isaiah 8:12–14; Isaiah 41:10

I sought the L<small>ORD</small>, and He heard me, and delivered me from all my fears.
—Psalm 34:4

For God has not given us a spirit of fear, but of power and of love and of a sound mind.
—2 Timothy 1:7

The enemy has worked tirelessly to "steal, kill, and destroy" me since birth. At three months old, I had to have two back surgeries. Mom and Dad noticed how painful it was for me to be given a bath. I would scream in discomfort every time Mom would bathe me. I can only imagine how unsettling this was for my parents as they navigated through the joys and fears of being first-time parents. They would soon find out from doctors that their newborn baby had been born with a small internal hole in my back. Doctors said the only thing keeping that hole from going all the way through to my spine was a piece of tissue the size of the tip of a ballpoint pen. Surgeons knew they needed to go in and repair that hole to decrease the possibility of spina bifida. So, in November 1974, at just three and a half months old, I underwent surgery to repair that hole. Many in the church where my dad served as the associate pastor and minister of music and youth came to be with Mom and Dad in the waiting room. Prayers were lifted up from all over the United States as people got word of the severity of my need. Those prayers caused all of heaven to move on my behalf, and the surgery was successful. It didn't take long, however, for this active little baby to kick the stitches loose and need a second back surgery. On top of all this, my right arm had to be put in traction because of how I had lain on it in the womb. Talk about high maintenance! Bless Mom and Dad's hearts! I firmly believe all this trauma from birth opened the door for the devil to send a "spirit of fear" to buffet me for much of my life.

Up until the age of thirty, I was paralyzed by fear. When I was a child, it manifested itself as shyness and the fear of disappointing others (perfectionism). As an adolescent, I could manage little to no independence and needed my parents for everything. However, in my twenties, I was confronted by this fear. I had already witnessed, as a preacher's kid, the battle against "the powers of this dark world and against the spiritual forces of evil in the heavenly realms" (Ephesians 6:12 NIV). I knew demons (evil spirits) existed, but they became very real to me when I began working as a prayer counselor at the 700 Club during college.

It started one night when the phones were busy with people from all over the world needing prayer. I was among at least two hundred more prayer counselors working that night when I received a call that shook me to my core. This "person" began speaking to me in a language with which I was unfamiliar. The voice was raspy and more like a growl as his voice increased in volume. As I prayed, he grew louder, drowning out my words; I then prayed louder and with more boldness. This went on until finally the caller hung up. I had been in a serious battle and was visibly shaken, but *whew!* It was over, and I was so thankful—until fifteen seconds later, when I received another call. It was the very same caller. Now, it would have been practically impossible for me to receive a call from the same "person," because he would've had to have somehow bypassed two hundred other counselors before reaching me again, but it happened, and he continued his chants—even speaking my name. I prayed with boldness in Jesus' name, but I wasn't as equipped as I should have been. "And these miracle signs will accompany those who believe: They will drive out demons in the power of my name. They will speak in tongues. They will be supernaturally protected from snakes and from drinking anything poisonous. And they will lay hands on the sick and heal them" (Mark 16:17–18 TPT).

As I matured—not only physically but spiritually, as

well—my fear subsided, or at least I thought it did. I was able to do things without my parents' constant help. I was singing with my sisters in churches and venues all over the country. I was talking one on one with people and learning how to communicate on my own. I was studying music in college, and I had discovered how to handle being told "no" and that I was not good enough, all the while still wanting to prove those people wrong. Confidence was creeping in, and it felt good!

I was never one who liked watching scary movies, but I still did it. I remember watching two popular horror movies from the late seventies and early eighties during that time in my life, and I had nightmares that seemed very real afterward. With each new year came movies that dug a little deeper to create terror in our lives. I knew this fear was not from my God (2 Timothy 1:7), but like many other people, I went along with the thrill of being scared out of my skin. Obviously, I ignored 1 Thessalonians 5:22 and its instruction to "reject every kind of evil." Those movies were not helping me keep my thoughts "fixed on all that is authentic and real, honorable and admirable, beautiful and respectful, pure and holy, merciful and kind. And fasten your thoughts on every glorious work of God, praising him always" (Philippians 4:8 TPT).

After eventually marrying a military man, my ability to take care of business on my own greatly improved. When you move thousands of miles away from your family of origin, and then your husband deploys, you are thrust into the ultimate state of independence, whether you like it or not. Again, I believed that fear no longer had a hold on me, and all was well. Smooth sailing from here on out, right? Not so much.

Many nights were spent alone in our little home on base, even though my husband made sure I had a companion to keep me company. Tilly, our German shepherd puppy, was the security I felt I needed. He was great—but not enough to keep away my night terrors. Yep! I started having night terrors that would frighten me out of sleep. Even when my husband wasn't away, I would wake up screaming, heart pounding and at the point of tears. There were many nights while sleeping that I would be awakened by the sound of my name being shouted. That eventually turned into me opening my eyes out of deep sleep to the appearance of "a person" standing in front of me shouting my name. No, this did not happen just once—but many times when I was in my late twenties. I would even jump over my husband in bed to get to the other side. This would usually wake my husband up in a sheer panic. This was not good.

After the birth of our firstborn son, and the diagnosis that brought us to our knees, I knew I had to get rid of this "spirit of fear." We were in the midst of a heavy battle for our son's life, and I could not be the warrior he needed if I was also being "buffeted" by my own evil spirit. So, as we learned more about our God through Scripture and His Holy Spirit, we realized we needed to walk in obedience no matter what we had been taught in the past. We had to step out of the "normal realm," get out of our comfort zone, and walk in truth, even if it felt uncomfortable. We had to walk in the supernatural Spirit of God: "If we live in the Spirit, let us also walk in the Spirit" (Galatians 5:25).

We began stepping out in faith looking for Holy Spirit-filled believers to stand with us and pray "the prayer that is said with faith" over our son (James 5:15). At one point, a mighty prayer warrior asked me if I was battling something myself. I felt a huge lump in my throat as I answered, "Yes, a spirit of fear." It was then that a group of bold prayer warriors laid hands on me, spoke the Word, and rebuked that spirit of fear from my life. There is no doubt in my mind that at that moment, I was delivered from the spirit of fear. A weight came off me, and I could breathe again. When they finished praying over me, I was commissioned to walk in faith, never to allow that spirit of fear to come in again. "For you did not receive the spirit of slavery to fall again into fear; rather, you received the Spirit of adoption, by whom we cry, 'Abba! Father!'" (Romans 8:15 TLV). Yes, it was up to me now. "Be sober, be vigilant; because your adversary the devil walks about like a roaring lion, seeking whom he may devour" (1 Peter 5:8). I could choose to open the door for him to come in again, or I could choose freedom: freedom from fear, freedom from terror, freedom from lack of approval, freedom from what might happen tomorrow, freedom from _____. You fill in the blank. "Now the Lord is the Spirit; and where the Spirit of the Lord is, there is liberty" (2 Corinthians 3:17).

I can honestly say that for the first time in my life, I was free to be what my God had called me to be. However, that doesn't necessarily mean the spirit of fear didn't try to take authority in my life again. It has tried. I can recall a time when my husband and I took a mini-vacay from the kids and went to San Antonio, Texas, for a work conference he needed to attend. As I walked the Riverwalk with another military spouse, I was confronted by a man I did not know. He said, "Hi, Tiffany" as I walked past him. His glaring eyes pierced my soul as he watched us walk out of sight. The friend I was with asked me if I knew him. I did not know the person, but I did recognize the source of the fear welling up inside of me. But this time I was confident in the authority I had. In Luke 10:19, Jesus' own words gave me that confidence: "Behold, I give you the authority to trample on serpents and scorpions, and over all the power of the enemy, and nothing shall by any means hurt you." I knew that "He who is in [me] is greater than he who is in the world" (1 John 4:4), and I truly believed it! I now choose each day to put on the "whole armor of God" (Ephesians 6:13–18): the "helmet of salvation" to protect my mind and thoughts (Philippians 4:6–7) and the "breastplate of righteousness" to protect my heart (Proverbs 4:23). Around my waist is the "belt of truth" from which I pull my weapon of offense, the "sword of the Spirit," which is the Word of God, and I hold tightly to the "shield of faith" to protect me from the enemy's fiery arrows. Then I put on the shoes of the Good News, which brings peace and keeps me firmly grounded in the midst of turmoil. Finally, to engage all this armor and these weapons of spiritual warfare, I must pray always in the Spirit. I must choose each day to leave no opening for the enemy to break through and wound the warrior. "And give no opportunity to the devil" (Ephesians 4:27 ESV).

I pray that today, as followers of Jesus Christ, we will "submit to God, resist the Devil" (James 4:7). May we walk in the light (1 John 1:7) so that evil will have no authority over us, in Jesus' name! "Choose today whom you will serve" (Joshua 24:15 NLT).

Revelation: Do not open the door to Satan to bring any "spirit of fear" into your life. Do not give place to the enemy. Dwell on the perfect love and promises of God.

MY GHOST STORY

WRITE DOWN WHAT THE HOLY SPIRIT SAYS TO YOU:

LESSON 20

The "Shade-y" Choice

Job 31:1; Matthew 5:28; 1 Corinthians 6:18–20; 1 Corinthians 10:13; Galatians 5:16; Colossians 3:5; 1 Thessalonians 4:3; 2 Timothy 2:22; Hebrews 13:4; James 1:14–15; 1 John 2:16

Help me turn my eyes away from illusions so that I pursue only that which is true; drench my soul with life as I walk in your paths.
—Psalm 119:37

Finally, brethren, whatever things are true, whatever things are noble, whatever things are just, whatever things are pure, whatever things are lovely, whatever things are of good report, if there is any virtue and if there is anything praiseworthy— meditate on these things.
—Philippians 4:8

I have *no* desire to see any of the *50 Shades* movies or any other sexually explicit films. I've seen what seemed to be godly marriages torn apart as a result of sexual immorality that first began with a quick look at something off-limits or "shady." That quick look then became unwholesome thoughts that led to more . . . fornication. The Greek word for *fornication* is where we get the English word "pornography." It is defined as "unlawful lust." It is also defined as "idolatry," and *idolatry* is defined as the "worship of idols" or "image worship." "Therefore, put to death what is earthly in you—sexual immorality, impurity, lust, evil desire, and greed—for that is idolatry" (Colossians 3:5 TLV). In its most basic form, fornication is not the physical act of sex. Fornication begins with what we look to and desire *above* the holiness to which we are called by almighty God. It starts with the eyes, proceeds to the mind, floods the heart, and *then* becomes the physical act of sex outside the sacred covenant of marriage between a husband and his wife. God calls that sin. You cannot convince me that anything good can come from an "innocent" glance, flirt, phone call, or text to someone other than my husband. There is a reason the Bible says to "flee" it (1 Corinthians 6:18)!

Ten years ago, I sat in a county courtroom, at the defendant's request, listening to testimony of how sex used in unwholesome and ungodly ways had led to bad consequences in her marriage and *all* involved in the immorality. The defendant was a woman who had been sexually abused in her younger years. Her life had been filled with men who were only interested in satisfying their own physical desires. Being used and abused was normal for her. That did not change with her second marriage. The endless cycle of feeling unworthy of real love—Christlike love—would only fuel the bad choices she would make that eventually brought her before the judge who would determine her future. The loss of her husband to suicide and a sentence of fifteen years in prison, away from her three-year-old daughter, would only be a small part of the consequences this woman would face for merely fulfilling her husband's perverted "requests." It was bondage she felt unable to escape, and it would imprison her for much of her life. The ramifications of her choices would be so serious that only the Spirit of the living God would be able to restore all that was lost. I was heartbroken for her, and I still pray for her and her daughter, to this very day as I write this. Heal her, O Lord, and she shall be healed. Save her, and she shall be saved, for You are my praise (see Jeremiah 17:14)!

I've witnessed how sex outside the covenant of marriage is the beginning of a free-for-all, boundary-less, self-serving attitude giving way to perversion and sexual addiction that can tear families apart, many of those families being inside the Church. The offender is never the only one affected. The spouse and children bear the almost-unbearable weight of the sexual disobedience. Healing and restoration can happen, but only through full repentance and the power of the Holy Spirit. However, the images seen and the deeds done leave lasting imprints that can never be removed. The lasting consequences reach far beyond the one who originally commits the sin. Sins will affect generation after generation if they are left unconfessed and un-repented of, and if the person is not restored by our heavenly Father. It is always best to flee sexual immorality of any kind. The Bible also calls this fornication. The Greek word used for "fornication" comes from a word meaning "harlotry." A harlot, or prostitute, has no honor or respect for the body the Lord gave her or him. The harlot exhibits no self-control with her or his own body. She/he is controlled by a "master" who also has no self-control over what he/she does. They are both slaves to their own unharnessed desires.

I believe there is so much confusion in the Church regarding sexual immorality, or fornication. I see it as taking control or authority over something that is not legally yours to control. Even an intimate touch by your boyfriend is him trespassing on private property, property that is owned by your Creator. Until a man and a woman unite in the covenant of marriage, intimate access to any part of God's "fearfully and wonderfully" made creation (Psalm 139:14) is off-limits.

Sexual immorality does not simply start with the physical act. The desires of the flesh always begin in the mind. Matthew 5:28 says, "But I say to you that whoever looks at a woman to lust for her has already committed adultery with her in his heart." The mind is the battleground where we either surrender to the temptations of the flesh or wield the weapons of the Spirit. We must make a choice before we go into battle every day. If we do not purpose to serve the Lord Jesus moment by moment, then we will allow the carnal thoughts to give way to acting in the heat of the moment. "I say then: Walk in the Spirit, and you shall not fulfill the lust of the flesh" (Galatians 5:16).

I've heard it said that "the eyes are the window to the soul." In Matthew 6:22–23, Jesus said, "The eye is the lamp of the body. Therefore if your eye is good, your whole body will be full of light. But if your eye is bad, your body will be full of darkness." In a world where images of sexual impurity are everywhere, keep your eyes fixed on the "light of the world" (John 9:5). Do not compromise for the "gray," but look to His bright glory and be set apart. "You are the salt of the earth; but if the salt loses its flavor, how shall it be seasoned? It is then good for nothing but to be thrown out and trampled underfoot by men. You are the light of the world. A city that is set on a hill cannot be hidden. Nor do they light a lamp and put it under a basket, but on a lampstand, and it gives light to all who are in the house. Let your light so shine before men, that they may see your good works and glorify your Father in heaven" (Matthew 5:13–16). The people of God do not live in the gray. We walk in the light of His countenance (Psalm 89:15). We walk as "children of light" (Ephesians 5:8). We are an unmistakable bright white for all the world to see. Be that light!

Remember also that we serve a God who gives grace,

and "if we walk in the light as He is in the light, we have fellowship with one another, and the blood of Jesus Christ His Son cleanses us from all sin" (1 John 1:7). Find accountability and confess, repent, and live free, people of God! Refuse the "gray," and keep your eyes fixed on Jesus (Hebrews 12:2).

Revelation: "Oh, be careful, little eyes, what you see. For the Father up above is looking down, with love. Oh, be careful, little eyes, what you see."

THE "SHADE-Y" CHOICE

WRITE DOWN WHAT THE HOLY SPIRIT SAYS TO YOU:

LESSON 21

Red and Yellow, Black and White

Genesis 1:26–27; Exodus 22:21; Leviticus 19:33–34; Proverbs 24:23; Matthew 28:19; John 7:24; John 13:34; Acts 17:26; Romans 2:11; Romans 10:12–13; 1 Corinthians 12:13; Galatians 3:28; Ephesians 4:32; Colossians 3:13; 1 Timothy 5:21; James 2:1; James 2:4; James 2:8–9; 1 John 2:11; 1 John 4:19–21; Revelation 7:9; Revelation 14:6

*"For the L*ORD *does not see as man sees; man looks on the outward appearance, but the L*ORD *looks on the heart."*
—1 Samuel 16:7

For there is no distinction between Jew and Greek, for the same Lord is Lord of all—richly generous to all who call on Him.
—Romans 10:12 TLV

> *Then Peter replied, "I see very clearly that God shows no favoritism. In every nation he accepts those who fear him and do what is right."*
> —**Acts 10:34–35** NLT

I've never understood thinking of myself better than someone else. I am part of the generation where every color was represented in my classrooms growing up. It was beautiful. Some of my closest relationships have been with people of a different color than me. Growing up in Florida, I was always the bright white and fair-skinned little girl on the beach with the fiery red hair. The bright white was because of all the sunscreen I was wearing. I definitely stood out in a crowd, and that is how I've been described my whole life . . . until now, when that fiery red hair has begun to lighten a little with each passing year.

My red hair and fair skin was the subject of much ridicule and name-calling early in my life. Names like "lava monster," "redheaded woodpecker," and "ugly" were just a few of the words used to describe me among peers. Most of the time, it was my dark-brown-skinned friends who stood up for me, and I will always be grateful for their courage and voice to stand up against unkindness. Honestly, for the first half of my life, I was tempted to believe everyone who was not fair-complexioned and redheaded were there to make fun of me, and I was especially a little scared of the blond-haired and blue-eyed "skater dudes," because they were the biggest perpetrators in the attacks on my self-worth. Nevertheless, as I formed relationships with those who had once seemed a threat, and as I matured in knowledge of who my God says I am, my heart softened. I began to see people more through Jesus' eyes, as well as the grace I was given, than through the the spirit of offense. "An understanding person demonstrates patience, for mercy means holding your tongue. When you are insulted, be quick to forgive and forget it, for you are virtuous when you overlook an offense" (Proverbs 19:11 TPT).

I understand this does not compare to the abuse and oppression that many people of different shades than me have experienced, but I was made very aware at an early age of the ugliness of people thinking they are better than another because of the color of their skin (or hair), or where they came from, or their education, or their career. No one is more important or valuable than another. We are all created for a purpose, and each one is very special. All of us who've been bought with the blood of Jesus and born of His Spirit should especially know this to be true. "There is neither Jew nor Greek, there is neither slave nor free, there is neither male nor female—for you are all one in Messiah Yeshua" (Galatians 3:28 TLV).

I'll never forget the time my youngest, Colt, described his beautiful and sweet babysitter, who was a teenager in our neighborhood, as "chocolate-skinned." I asked him to describe my skin, and he said, "Vanilla." He loved ice cream, and his descriptions matched the innocence of his heart. He knew we all looked a little different in shades of color, but he also knew that he loved his babysitter and thought she *hung the moon*. Colt did not describe people as simply "black" and "white." He seemed to describe folks as crayon colors. While I had been labeled a "redhead" my whole life, Colt saw my hair as "orange" because it matched his orange crayon better. He loved to make beautiful pictures with all the different-colored crayons. He didn't like to color with just black and white—he wanted *all* the colors. It made the picture that much more beautiful. Isn't that like our God? He made all the colors, so why not use them when He created us in His image?

My Jesus was part of an ethnic group who were abused, horribly mistreated, enslaved, and murdered. "He was despised and rejected by men, a man of deep sorrows who was no stranger to suffering and grief. We hid our faces from him in disgust and considered him a nobody, not worthy of respect" (Isaiah 53:3 TPT). Those of us who have been bought with His precious blood should count Him worthy of all respect. Since Jesus offered His body "once for *all*" (Hebrews 10:10), should we not consider *all* people worthy of respect? In 2 Corinthians 5:16–17, Paul tells the Church to "refuse to evaluate people merely by their outward appearances. For that's how we once viewed the Anointed One, but no longer do we see him with limited human insight. Now, if anyone is enfolded into Christ, he has become an entirely new person. All that is related to the old order has vanished. Behold, everything is fresh and new." If we are a new creature in Christ, we are to regard no one as unworthy of love and respect. Though the culture said otherwise, Jesus did not regard those from a different ethnic group to be unworthy (John 4:9–10). Jesus did not regard females as unworthy (Galatians 3:28). Our Lord did not consider the young or old unworthy (1 Timothy 4:12 and 5:1–2), and our God definitely does not look on the outward appearance (1 Samuel 16:6–7). "Therefore be *imitators* of God as dear children" (Ephesians 5:1). Let us imitate Jesus in how we see and treat others.

The abundant life our Lord Jesus offers is for *all* who come to Him by faith (John 10:10). Our goal and our message should be the same. I'm praying we all get to know the Savior of the world in a deep way and learn to love each other as He loves us. We are all part of the human race. We all bleed the same, and we are all offered the same redeeming precious blood of Jesus Christ so that "whoever believes in Him should not perish but have everlasting life" (John 3:16).

Revelation: See everyone through the eyes of Jesus.

WRITE DOWN WHAT THE HOLY SPIRIT SAYS TO YOU:

LESSON 22

What's in a Name?

Genesis 27:36; 1 Samuel 25:25; Matthew 28:19; Revelation 3:12

Lift up your eyes on high, and see! Who created these? The One who brings out their host by number, the One who calls them all by name. Because of His great strength and vast power, not one is missing.

—Isaiah 40:26

"To him the doorkeeper opens, and the sheep hear his voice. The shepherd calls his own sheep by name and leads them out."

—John 10:3

Family time is fun time. When the boys' cousins, especially their third cousins who are similar in age, come to visit, we experience a lot of Nerf gun wars, football games, and video game playing. One particular gathering included a conversation about their names. So, that night after supper, we began to research each name's meaning. One name meant "merciful, mild, and gentle." Another name meant "pure and clean," and there was one whose name meant "full of heart." There was another whose name meant "man," and one whose name meant "holy one." As we discovered the meaning of each of their names, we could see a sense of dignity stirring up in each young man. Until . . . the last name we looked up had the meaning of "charcoal town." "Charcoal town"? That wasn't much of a badge of honor for this young man. In fact, he was rather discouraged about it, so we decided to look up his middle name, which meant "valiant." That still brought no comfort. So, the cousin whose name meant "man" came to the rescue, offering a great explanation of the many benefits of charcoal. Now, the one whose name meant "charcoal town" will also be known as the "valiant" one who "fuels the most intense fire, heals, and filters out all the bad stuff"! That was the encouragement needed to help this young man feel honorable again. "Therefore encourage one another and build each other up—just as you in fact are doing" (1 Thessalonians 5:11 TLV). All is well. Thanks, "man"!

Do you know that the Most High God calls *you* by name? He takes great pleasure in calling your name and encouraging you. "For Jacob My servant's sake, and Israel My elect, I have even called you by your name; I have named you, though you have not known Me" (Isaiah 45:4). Even before we knew Him, He called us by name. The beginning of Isaiah 45, verse 1, says, "Thus says the

WHAT'S IN A NAME?

Lord to His anointed . . ." This Scripture is God speaking directly to King Cyrus to fulfill a certain purpose, "that you may know that I, the Lord, who call you by your name, am the God of Israel" (Isaiah 45:3). Don't you think those who have been born again are called to fulfill a similar purpose so that the world will "know" that He is God? Are we not anointed to make our God known throughout the world? "But you have an anointing from the Holy One, and you all know" (1 John 2:20 TLV). He calls us by name so that we will recognize that anointing and walk in the purpose for which He named us. That should give each of us a sense of honor and dignity.

Another beautiful thing our heavenly Father does is call us according to the work finished through Jesus Christ. He no longer calls us "slave." He calls us "son" (Galatians 4:7). He no longer calls us "servant." He calls us "friend" (John 15:15). We are no longer a "foreigner and stranger," but we are a "citizen" and a "member of the household of God" (Ephesians 2:19). We are now clothed in His righteousness through Jesus! A holy God has to see us through the blood of Jesus Christ. Therefore, He no longer sees the old. He sees the new (Romans 3:20–26). Praise God!

Names are very important to our God. *Abram* became *Abraham*, meaning "father of a multitude" (Genesis 17:5), and *Sarai* became *Sarah*, meaning "mother of nations" (Genesis 17:15). The promise of God to make Abraham "a father of many nations" would be carried out under these new names. Paul used the Hebrew name *Saul* when he was persecuting Christians, and later, after his conversion and when he began to believe in and preach Jesus Christ, he chose to be called by his Roman name, *Paul*, in order to reach the Gentiles (Romans 11:13). These name changes reflect a new identity given for God's honor and glory. In essence, the new name shifted the person into their God-given purpose. Sure, the devil wants us to think we are living under the same old name. He likes to place doubts in our minds about our true identity in Christ and the purpose for which we were created. Don't allow him to do that.

As far as birth names, another observation I've made in my walk with the Holy Spirit is that my heavenly Father always calls me by my full first name, *Tiffany*, meaning "revelation of God." He never calls me "Tiff," "Tippy," or any other nicknames given by family or friends. He seems to take our names seriously, and He is intentional with how He addresses us when He speaks.

On the other hand, the enemy is often more "flattering" with how he talks to us. He wants to deceive us into thinking he's our buddy, so he'll frequently use nicknames. He is the father of lies, and he will stop at nothing to make you think he's got your best interest at heart. Be wise and recognize the difference between what Satan calls you and what the Lord Most High calls you.

Let's look more closely at our identity in Christ Jesus:

FREE
Psalm 146:7; John 8:32; John 8:36; Romans 8:2; Galatians 5:1; Galatians 5:13

FORGIVEN/FORGIVING
Psalm 103:3; Matthew 6:14; Romans 8:1; Ephesians 1:7; Ephesians 4:32; Colossians 2:13; Colossians 3:13; James 5:15; 1 John 1:9; 1 John 2:12

HEALED
Psalm 103:3; Psalm 107:20; Psalm 147:3; Isaiah 53:5; Jeremiah 33:6; 1 Peter 2:24

SAVED
Ephesians 2:8; 1 Thessalonians 5:9

BLESSED BY GOD
Jeremiah 29:11; Galatians 3:14; 3 John 2

RIGHTEOUSNESS OF GOD
Romans 6:18, 22; 3:22; 2 Corinthians 5:21

CHILDREN/SONS AND DAUGHTER OF GOD
John 1:12–13; Galatians 3:26; Romans 8:15

FRIENDS OF GOD
John 15:15

SALT AND LIGHT
Matthew 5:13–16; Matthew 13:43

JUSTIFIED
Romans 2:13; 3:24; 5:1; James 2:24

RECONCILED TO GOD
Romans 5:11

RECONCILERS
2 Corinthians 5:18

HAVING ACCESS TO GOD
Romans 5:2; Ephesians 3:12

SERVANT TO ALL
1 Corinthians 9:19

NEW CREATION
2 Corinthians 5:17

CONQUERORS/VICTORS/OVERCOMERS
Romans 8:37; 1 Corinthians 15:57; 1 John 4:4

BONDSERVANTS OF GOD
1 Peter 2:16

PEOPLE OF LOVE
John 15:12; 1 John 4:11; 1 John 4:7, 12; Ephesians 3:12, 17; 5:2

DELIVERED
Philippians 1:19 nkjv

PEACEFUL, GENTLE, HUMBLE
Philippians 4:7; Titus 3:2

AMBASSADORS FOR CHRIST
2 Corinthians 5:20

SANCTIFIED
Hebrews 10:10; 2 Timothy 2:21

BEING MADE COMPLETE/PERFECTED
Hebrews 13:21; Philippians 1:6

CREATED FOR GOOD WORKS/HIS MASTERPIECE
Psalm 139:14; 1 Peter 2:5; 2 Timothy 3:17

WITNESSES
Acts 1:8

CALLED/CHOSEN/PRIEST/HOLY/SPECIAL
1 Peter 2:9; Colossians 3:12; 1 Thessalonians 5:24

JOINT HEIRS WITH JESUS
Romans 8:17

DISCIPLES
John 8:31

LOVE FOR ONE ANOTHER
John 13:35

REDEEMED
Lamentations 3:58; Psalm 107:2; Isaiah 43:1; Luke 1:68; Galatians 3:13; Ephesians 1:7; Colossians 1:14; 1 Peter 1:18–19

FAITH-FILLED LIFE
Galatians 2:20; 2 Corinthians 5:7

HIDDEN/SAFE/SECURE
Colossians 3:3; Psalm 91:1, 4

ADORED/BELOVED/LOVED
John 3:16; Ephesians 2:4; 1 John 4:10; John 15:13

If you've been bought with the blood of Jesus and received His free gift of salvation through faith, then being called by any name contrary to these is not of God. Remind the devil of your identity in Christ Jesus and watch him flee. Only declare what almighty God declares. Let us not cheapen Jesus' precious sacrifice by allowing our tongues to call ourselves names that negate the blood and body broken for us by the spotless Lamb of God.

Revelation: Call yourself only by the names given to you by almighty God. Jesus paid much too high a price for you to believe you are less than who He says you are. The devil has no legal right to give you a different name when you are a child of the King.

WHAT'S IN A NAME?

WRITE DOWN WHAT THE HOLY SPIRIT SAYS TO YOU:

LESSON 23

Playing Second Fiddle

Micah 6:8; Proverbs 11:2; Matthew 22:37–39; Matthew 23:12; Mark 9:35; Mark 10:45; Luke 14:11; Romans 12:3; Ephesians 4:2; Philippians 2:3–8; Colossians 1:18; Colossians 3:12; 1 Peter 5:5–6; James 3:13; James 3:17–18; James 4:6; 1 John 4:19

*By humility and the fear of the L*ORD *are riches and honor and life.*
—Proverbs 22:4

"The last will be first, and the first will be last."
—Matthew 20:16 NIV

Do nothing out of selfish ambition or vain conceit. Rather, in humility value others above yourselves, not looking to your own interests but each of you to the interests of the others.
—Philippians 2:3–4 NIV

"She plays second fiddle to no one." These are the words from someone in the church describing another believer, who also happens to be one of the lead singers on the "praise team." This grieved me. If anyone should be willing to "play second fiddle," it should be the person leading the congregation in singing praises to the One who "humbled Himself and became obedient to the point of death, even the death of the cross," as Paul describes Jesus in his letter to the church at Philippi. Unfortunately, this is not the case for many up on the platform today. I had seen firsthand this lady's lack of humility in her "welcome," or lack thereof, of a newcomer on the praise team. This should not be happening in the body of Christ. I know this man was speaking figuratively about this person, but the more I pondered on it, instead of anger, I felt sad for anyone who "plays second fiddle to no one."

I've played first fiddle and second fiddle, both literally and figuratively, and I have benefited from doing both. There's a lot of pressure playing first fiddle (or, violin, in my case). The music can be a bit more challenging. Sometimes there are many more notes to play, the notes move faster, and the music somehow ends up in the stratosphere where only dogs can hear. Technically, it can be more difficult, which is why you want some of your best players playing first violin. In a symphony, first violinists play some of the most familiar and beautiful melodies. Obviously, because of all these things, first "fiddlers" get more of the praise and attention. They are out front, closest to the audience, for all to see.

PLAYING SECOND FIDDLE

However, I *love* playing second violin. Tucked safely inside the orchestra, I could relax a bit and enjoy the music around me. I'm not focused on being seen, and I'm not even concerned as much about singularly being heard. Instead, playing second violin actually places me in a position of listening to the orchestra as a whole. I can hear the violas and the cellos, who have some of the deepest and richest tones in the orchestra. I can see the woodwinds better as they blow into their instruments and make beautiful music, and I can definitely better hear the sounds of the brass as they play all their fanfares. For one reason or another, playing "second fiddle" helps me better focus on the conductor. I believe it's because I'm not as distracted by the audience looking at me. I also love playing those beautiful harmonies. Sometimes the seconds play the familiar recognizable melodies along with the firsts, but most of the time they are playing the harmony part. That harmony is what really adds flavor and draws the hearer into the musical piece. Dissonances that resolve to consonances, themes that give color to the musical story . . . I could go on and on. Needless to say, second fiddle is very important!

This appreciation for second fiddle didn't come until I was older, though. In my early schooling years, first fiddle was where you wanted to be as an overachieving student concerned about your status in class. As I grew in maturity, though, I knew there needed to be a second fiddle in order to create beautiful music. The pressure was off to impress the teacher and other students. It wasn't about me any longer. It was about the bigger picture. It was about helping to create a beautiful symphony of praise under the authority of the Master Conductor.

With this understanding comes humility, which, I believe, those who never play second fiddle will ever have the benefit of learning. Humility should be in the description of every true follower of Jesus Christ. What does humility and putting other above ourselves do? Scripture tells us in Philippians 2 that it encourages others, and it comforts others in Jesus' love. When we walk in humility, we share in the fellowship of the Spirit, and in mercy and compassion we make our joy complete by being of the "same mind, having the same love, united in spirit, with one purpose" (verse 2 TLV). Humility is key to edifying the Church. We are most effective when we work together in one accord to show Jesus to the world.

Yes, there are those who have spent time in the very challenging and refining "first fiddle" section, but there should always be a time when we step away from the first position and give others the opportunity to be challenged. The fruitful evidence of playing both first and second will be such a beautiful masterpiece that others will want the same for their own lives. James 3:13 in *The Passion Translation* says: "If you consider yourself to be wise and one who understands the ways of God, advertise it with a beautiful, fruitful life guided by wisdom's gentleness. Never brag or boast about what you've done, and you'll prove that you're truly wise." The temptation for those who have been the object of everyone's attention is to stay there. When we remain in that position of being first, we lose sight of the whole ensemble. We stop listening to others, and we become distracted from focusing on the Conductor, the One who gave us the talent in the first place. We could learn a lot from playing second fiddle . . . or viola . . . but that's a whole other lesson for another day.

Revelation: If we are to work together to proclaim Jesus to the world, we need every gift, every talent, every calling, every unique instrument to create a beautiful symphony of praise to the Lord. No one is any less special. All are needed and very important.

WRITE DOWN WHAT THE HOLY SPIRIT SAYS TO YOU:

_____
_____
_____
_____
_____
_____
_____
_____
_____
_____
_____
_____
_____
_____
_____
_____
_____
_____
_____
_____

LESSON 24

"It's Not a Kai-Peeper!"

Ecclesiastes 5:2–3; Ecclesiastes 10:12; Ezekiel 47:9; Proverbs 12:25; Proverbs 13:3; Proverbs 15:1, 4; Proverbs 16:24; Proverbs 18:4; Proverbs 18:21; Proverbs 31:8; Ephesians 4:29; Colossians 3:17; Colossians 4:5–6; James 1:1

> *Reckless speech is like the thrusts of a sword, but the tongue of the wise brings healing.*
> —**Proverbs 12:18** TLV

Love is large and incredibly patient. Love is gentle and consistently kind to all. It refuses to be jealous when blessing comes to someone else. Love does not brag about one's achievements nor inflate its own importance. Love does not traffic in shame and disrespect, nor selfishly seek its own honor. Love is not easily irritated or quick to take offense. Love joyfully celebrates honesty and finds no delight in what is wrong. Love is a safe place of shelter, for it never stops believing the best for others. Love never

takes failure as defeat, for it never gives up.
—**1 Corinthians 13:4–8** TPT

I absolutely *love* this Scripture in *The Passion Translation*. I would love to tell you that I've been faithful to fulfill every one of these descriptions of what love is, but I have missed the mark many times. This is especially true when I am tired and weary.

Have you ever said something and immediately wished you could rewind the tape and shut the hatch? Yep! Me too!

Much like the mother of a newborn baby, mothers of extraordinary kids have sleepless nights. *Unlike* the mother of a newborn baby, however, our child is much bigger with all the needs of any other young adult, and more. We continue to bathe, clothe, feed, brush teeth, and completely take care of all those needs. If our extraordinary young adult has difficulty verbalizing his or her specific needs and wants, it can become even more exhausting mentally and emotionally. We are problem-solving all day to figure out what is hurting or causing aggravation for our child. It requires a lifelong commitment and can take a toll on us, especially if there is no rest.

Even so, there is never a good reason to lose control and lash out at someone. One such emotional outburst happened when Shad, Clem, and I were settling into our new home in Maryland. Colt, our youngest, had not yet been born. We had just moved there from Enid, Oklahoma,

"IT'S NOT A KAI-PEEPER!"

and we had spent some time living in our fifth-wheel while in the process of purchasing our new home in Maryland. So, I was ready to get settled into a place where we were not bumping into each other all day. However, Clemmie loved the fifth-wheel. He loved the tight, intimate space. After we settled into our new home, Shad built a parking pad for our camper right next to the house, so Clemmie was excited. He could see it. He could touch it, and he could go inside his "Kai-peeper." That is what Clem called it, and we were grateful for that word from him . . . any word from him! It was music to our ears . . . except for that one time.

Like all the "lessons" in the book, this was a time when the Holy Spirit taught and brought to remembrance His Word: "May my teaching trickle like rain, my speech distill like dew—like gentle rain on new grass, like showers on tender plants" (Deuteronomy 32:2 TLV). This particular moment, my "teaching" was more like a monsoon than a gentle rain. We had been in the car coming home from a little road trip. Clemmie had the camper on his mind. It was a place of solitude and peace for him. He had been asking for the "kai-peeper" on repeat for a while on the trip. Finally, my patience had come to an end, and with heightened intensity, I exclaimed, "It's not a kai-peeper! It's a CAM-per!" For a moment, it seemed that my brash response had quieted the inquisition. But I felt shame. I then softened my tone and began to gently teach Clem the word: "cam-per." "Cam-per"—"slow it down, Clem, and say 'cam-per'." He gave me his very best efforts as he continued to ask for the camper until we returned home.

Aren't we so thankful that our heavenly Father is patient with His children? He doesn't shout at us or storm off in a rage. No. In fact, He is gentle and compassionate toward us. "'The LORD, the LORD God, merciful and gracious, longsuffering, and abounding in goodness and truth'" (Exodus 34:6). Our God is "rich in mercy, because of His great love with which He loved us . . . made us alive together with Christ . . . that in the ages to come He might show the exceeding riches of His grace in His kindness toward us in Christ Jesus" (Ephesians 2:4–7). He is so gracious and longsuffering toward His children, even when we repeat the same question over and over again (2 Peter 3:9). Because He is holy and "there is no unrighteousness in Him" (Psalm 92:15), His words and actions are always used to produce what is beneficial for His people . . . body, soul, and spirit. Proverbs 30:5 (TLV) says, "Every word of God is purified. He is a shield to those who take refuge in Him." Our heavenly Father's will is to bless, defend, protect, encourage, and heal. Why would we want to be any different in word and in deed? We shouldn't be. When we understand the power in our words, we will be more thoughtful and intentional in how we use them. "Pleasant words are like a honeycomb, sweetness to the soul and health to the bones" (Proverbs 16:24). When we understand the consequences of our actions, or reactions, we will be less likely to throw a fit in anger. "A hot-tempered man stirs up strife, but one who is slow to anger calms a quarrel"

(Proverbs 15:18). Isn't our heart's desire to heal and not to hurt? It should be because that is the heart of God for His children, and I know that is my heart's desire for my children.

The Lord God does not ask us to be anything He Himself is not. On the contrary, He tells us to "be *imitators of God* as dear children. And walk in love, as Christ also has loved us and given Himself for us, an offering and a sacrifice to God for a sweet-smelling aroma" (Ephesians 5:1–2). Scripture even goes so far as to tell us to "be holy" as He is holy (Leviticus 11:44–45; 19:2; 20:7, 26; Numbers 15:40; Ephesians 1:4; 5:27; 1 Peter 1:15–16). It seems like an impossible task, doesn't it? If we didn't serve and surrender to the God of the impossible, I would agree (Jeremiah 32:27; Matthew 19:26; Mark 10:27; Luke 1:37). But our God does the impossible to those who simply believe Him (Mark 9:23). If we believe we cannot be holy, then we will live accordingly, but if we truly believe what the Word of God says, we will submit to His authority and walk in the fullness of His glory. We must know His Word and then surrender to His Spirit in order to be the "consecrated" people He wants us to be (1 Peter 1:16).

James 1:19 (TLV) says, "Know this, my dear brothers and sisters: let every person be quick to listen, slow to speak, and slow to anger." Self-control is evidence of the Holy Spirit in us. If we have trouble restraining our emotions and our tongues, then we need to submit to His authority instead of our own flesh. Reactive speech is not self-control. Parents, when we have moments like this, our children need to see repentance. In Scripture, the most used definition for the word *repentance* is μετάνοια, which means "to reverse your way of thinking, reform, reverse." When we repent, we need to reverse what has been done and change direction so that it is not done again. Stop making excuses for bad behavior, get in His Word, and walk in the Spirit of God. Finally, "let your speech always be gracious, seasoned with salt, so that you may know how you ought to answer each person" (Colossians 4:6). I apologized to Clemmie, and, as always, he was so gracious to forgive Mommy, put a smile on his face, and remind me of how beautiful his precious life is. I continue to learn so much from my son. Thank you, Clemmie! Thank You, Lord!

Revelation: Our words are like deep waters. They can either drown those around us, or our words can be a river of life that makes the lame to walk and the blind to see, that opens prison doors and sets the captives free. Spring up, O Well!

"IT'S NOT A KAI-PEEPER!"

WRITE DOWN WHAT THE HOLY SPIRIT SAYS TO YOU:

LESSON 25

That's Good Enough

Psalm 103:1; Proverbs 13:4; Proverbs 16:3; Matthew 5:16; Matthew 25:40; Luke 19:46; Romans 14:6–8; 1 Corinthians 10:31; Galatians 1:10; Galatians 6:9; Ephesians 3:21; Ephesians 6:6–7; Colossians 3:17, 24; 1 Peter 4:11

> *"In all that he did in the service of the Temple of God and in his efforts to follow God's laws and commands, Hezekiah sought his God wholeheartedly. As a result, he was very successful."*
> **—2 Chronicles 31:21** NLT

> *Put your heart and soul into every activity you do, as though you are doing it for the Lord himself and not merely for others. For we know that we will receive a reward, an inheritance from the Lord, as we serve the Lord YAHWEH, the Anointed One!*
> **—Colossians 3:23–24** TPT

The Church used to be the place for learning not just Scripture, but song and music. It seems as though, in this *American Idol*/fast food/got-to-have-it now culture, we are content with "that's good enough." We refuse to put in the time and effort to make something better and learn. We are seeing the consequences of this in our local churches, and I do not believe that pleases the Lord, who desires our firstfruits. "By His will, He brought us forth by the word of truth, so that we might be a kind of firstfruits of all He created" (James 1:18 TLV).

In 1978 (before YouTube, Facebook, or any other social media outlet), after singing my first public solo in front of a thousand congregants, I quickly realized I had a passion for music. It really became the Lord's way of giving me purpose and bringing me out of my redheaded insecurities. It was not just something I loved and was passionate about, but I also seemed to be good at it. From a very young age, I became a student of music. I knew where the center of the pitch was, and I knew when to come in at the right time without help. I could hear harmonies. I memorized music easily and worked to learn as much about it as possible. I played instruments by ear. It did not take long for me to realize that music was what I loved, and I quickly came to realize that music ministry was what God was calling me to do in order to build His Kingdom and glorify His name.

After I understood the talent, and the calling, I did not want to bury it or hide it (Matthew 25:18). I wanted to nurture it and grow it (Matthew 25:21). My desire was to show my Jesus that I was thankful for what *He* had given. In high school, I studied music and focused on playing the violin. I then went on to study and earn a degree in music from one of the best colleges of music in the United States. My goal was to earn a degree in vocal performance. Singing was what I was truly passionate about and what I had been doing since I was four years old. This turned out to be a more difficult task than I had originally imagined. The vocal professors did not welcome me with open arms. In fact, they discouraged me and told me I was not vocal performance–ready. I did not run away or get offended at being told I was "not good enough," and there has been plenty of that. The vocal professors at the College of Music were convinced that I did not belong as a vocal performance major. After all, I had been in orchestras, playing my violin, throughout my high school years. Unlike all the other vocal performance majors, I had no vocal teacher in high school through which I came highly recommended. I had no all-state vocal awards like most of the other vocal performance majors had earned. According to them, I was not equipped to be a professional classical singer. I had been singing professionally in the Southern Gospel music world for years before I went to college. I was challenged to commit fully to become a classical singer, learning how to sing correctly in order to *steward* my voice well. We are to want to be good stewards of what God gives us. All this opposition made me want to do better and work harder.

To me, the calling was not only to be nurtured and

matured through training in school, but the anointing needed to be there, too. That was given out of full submission to the Holy Spirit's work in me and through some really tough times of brokenness. Just because you can *sing* does not mean you have the calling, and just because you have the calling doesn't necessarily mean you have the anointing . . . yet. I believe our God is saying, *Are you serious about this? Are you willing to be obedient with what I've given you and use it for My glory? Can I trust you with it?*

The body of Christ should not be the place for "that's good enough" worship. It's time to stop *just* showing up to worship together. Does a bride "just show up" for her wedding? No, she spends months, if not longer, preparing for the wedding. She spends money on the cake, the venue, the food, the musicians, the flowers, and the beautiful white dress. She spends hours putting on her makeup and doing her hair. She sometimes spends weeks and months making sure she eats healthier so that she will fit into that beautiful white dress on which she spent lots of money. The bride does all this to prepare to see her groom. She does all this to present her very best to the one she loves. What if the Bride of Christ were to prepare the same way for her Bridegroom, "that He might sanctify and cleanse her with the washing of water by the word, that He might present her to Himself a glorious church, not having spot or wrinkle or any such thing, but that she should be holy and without blemish" (Ephesians 5:26–27)? That is the Church the world needs to see. Who wouldn't want to be part of that celebration?

We need to prepare our hearts, our minds, our music, and our message to reverently come into the presence of the One True God, expecting that He will bless our preparation. We cannot hold back in giving *all* our gifts and talents back to the One who gave them to us. We cannot be stingy with our offerings. The Old Testament contains many examples of the Lord requiring the firstfruits and our very best offerings. In the New Testament, I think of the story of Ananias and Sapphira, a husband and wife who sold a piece of land. Because they were stingy and lied about bringing all of the money back to the Lord, they were judged—and caused to drop dead. What if the Church today is being judged by how we hold back from giving our best to the Lord? I believe our God would "open the windows of Heaven and pour out for [us] such blessing that there will not be room enough to receive it" (Malachi 3:10). We must spur one another on to, first, use the gifts and talents we've each been given, in the right place, at the right time, and, second, grow, mature, and continue to learn how to bring our very best before Almighty God . . . our "first fruits." My heart breaks to see the "good enough" in our worship services, whether it be in our tithes, our offerings, our musical praise, our preaching, or our praying. We must do better.

Abba Father, open our eyes to see our individual callings in Your Church. Let us not only recognize the calling, but also take it seriously. May we nurture and grow the gifts and talents You've given us so that we can be supernaturally effective to lead a lost world to You. May we not be comfortable or complacent, nor settle for not bringing our very best to You. May we teach our children and youth to grow deeper so that they will experience true worship of You in their lives. We love You, Father. In Jesus' name, amen!

Revelation: Our God deserves our very best, not our "good enough." Give it all to Jesus!

WRITE DOWN WHAT THE HOLY SPIRIT SAYS TO YOU:

LESSON 26

Stuck Between Walls

Psalm 32:7; Psalm 91; Psalm 121:5–8; Psalm 140:4; Proverbs 2:11; Proverbs 7:2; Proverbs 16:17; Romans 6:12; Galatians 5:16, 24; Ephesians 2:3; Philippians 4:7; 1 Peter 1:14; 1 John 2:16

> *Like a dog that returns to its vomit,*
> *so a fool repeats his folly.*
> **—Proverbs 26:11** TLV

> *But these people are like irrational animals—*
> *creatures of instinct born to be captured and killed.*
> *They malign what they don't understand, and in*
> *their destruction they will be utterly destroyed.*
> **—2 Peter 2:12** TLV

What do you do when your eighty-pound German shepherd gets stuck in between the hangar metal panels and the storeroom wall? Jessi Lou had been chasing our barn cat and found herself in a tight spot. She was forced to stay in that tight spot for at least an hour or more until I finally noticed she was nowhere to be found and began my search for her. I looked everywhere I thought she liked to go on the farm. I yelled her name, thinking she would come running back to me. Finally, I heard movement in the walls of the hangar and her very quiet whimper. Jessi needed to be rescued because her animal instincts had led her into trouble. She was trapped.

Thankfully, I had a brave ten-year-old son, who grabbed his flashlight and went in between the walls, where the scorpions and rattlesnakes were, in order to rescue her. You see, Colt loved his dog, and he was willing to take the risks involved to save her. Unfortunately for Jessi-Lou, Colt was not yet physically equipped to get her out of that tight spot. He needed longer arms and the ability to lift at least twice his weight. He felt helpless and sad that his attempts failed. That is when I placed a call to Uncle "Owl," who jumped in his car to drive the hour and twenty minutes to help. Uncle Al, Shad's older brother, knew the terrain. He had been there when PawPaw had built the hangar, and he was well aware of the distance between the walls. He was stronger, and he had experience pulling longhorns out of the brush and other things in which their horns would get entangled. Freeing an eighty-pound German shepherd would not be too hard for him. He was also always willing to help, especially when Shad was away on a trip. By the time Uncle Al arrived, MawMaw had already phoned a friend who engaged with a young man at the local volunteer fire department. This young man was just the right size and had all the right training and tools to pull Jessi back to freedom. Knowing how dogs can be, Uncle "Owl" made the most of his trip and fabricated a barrier the cat could climb through, but the dog could not. The rescue mission was a success not only to *free* Jessi from bondage, but to *keep* her *out* of bondage.

Jessi Lou was following her primal instincts when she tried to chase the cat. The cat could escape out of small spaces, but the dog could not. However, Jessi was not concerned with the consequences of her actions. She just wanted that cat. How many times do we, like Jessi Lou, follow our *natural* instincts and find ourselves stuck between a rock and a hard place? Are we chasing something that we know will lead us into bondage? Have we received help out of that bondage only to return to what got us in trouble in the first place? Like Jessi Lou, we tend to follow our natural instincts and go after what our flesh desires and the things that entrap us. Like Jessi, we tend to be creatures of habit, again pursuing what easily ensnares us.

It took three people to help in rescuing Jessi that day, and each one mirrored the heart of our God in rescuing us from sin and death. Colt showed the depth of his *love* for his dog by going down into that dark, critter-infested, tight spot. He had the heart to free her, but he needed the physical body that was required to actually *complete* the rescue. The strong, young volunteer firefighter physically fulfilled that requirement. Then, Uncle Al came along and *sealed* the deal to *keep* her out of captivity. Doesn't this sound familiar? God the Father, because of His great love for us, sent His only begotten Son, Jesus, in human form to rescue us from the dark, serpent-infested pit. Furthermore, He sent His Holy Spirit to seal us and keep us out for the day of His return.

Unlike Jessi Lou, we have been created in the "image of God" (Genesis 1:27). We are image bearers, with a choice to make: follow the Good Shepherd (John 10) or follow the "tempter" (Matthew 4:3; 1 Thessalonians 3:5). Unlike Jessi, we have been given a new nature (Colossians 3:10), one that leads to freedom (John 8:32; Galatians 5:1) and life abundant (John 10:10). Scripture tells us to "get rid of every weight and entangling sin" (Hebrews 12:1 TLV). If we are truly a "new creation" (2 Corinthians 5:17) in Christ Jesus, bought with His blood, and clothed in His righteousness, why then would we continue to be led by our own desires? "Are we to continue in sin so that grace may abound? May it never be!" (Romans 6:1–2 TLV). The truth is that grace "teaches us to say, 'No'" to our fleshly desires (Titus 2:11–13), and we have the fruit of self-control through the power of the Holy Spirit in us (Galatians 5:23). We have also been *sealed* by His Spirit (Ephesians 4:30), who is also able to *keep* us from stumbling (Jude 1:24).

Certainly, we are confident in our Helper, but we should also be confident in His promise to always "provide a way of escape" (1 Corinthians 10:13 TLV). He has also provided a safeguard, His Spirit, to keep us out of trouble, but we must not follow our own fleshly desires; rather, we must keep our eyes fixed on Jesus, "the author and finisher of our faith" (Hebrews 12:2). I'm so very grateful that almighty God sent Jesus to rescue me out of the clutches of sin and death, and then He sent the Holy Spirit to keep me out of that trouble. Thank You, Lord! "God, you're such a safe and powerful place to find refuge! You're a proven help in time of trouble—more than enough and always available whenever I need you" (Psalm 46:1 TPT).

 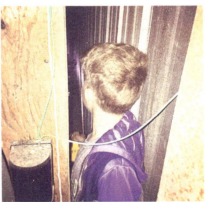

Jessi Lou stuck between the hangar and storeroom walls.

Revelation: Almighty God is our help in times of trouble. Walk in His Spirit to remain secure, stable, and free in full assurance of His leading and care.

FEELS SO GOOD TO LAY DOWN

WRITE DOWN WHAT THE HOLY SPIRIT SAYS TO YOU:

LESSON 27

Pick Up Trash or Pick Flowers... Your Choice

Proverbs 10:31; Proverbs 12:14; Proverbs 13:3; Proverbs 15; Proverbs 21:23; Proverbs 25:11; Proverbs 25:25; Matthew 15:11, 18; Romans 10:10; James 1:26; James 3:10; 1 Peter 3:10

Death and life are in the power of the tongue, and those who love it will eat its fruit.
—**Proverbs 18:21**

"But I say to you that for every idle word men may speak, they will give account of it in the day of judgment. For by your words you will be justified, and by your words you will be condemned."
—**Matthew 12:36–37**

Let no corrupt word proceed out of your mouth, but

> *what is good for necessary edification, that it may impart grace to the hearers.*
> **—Ephesians 4:29**

If your words had the power to create, would you create a beautiful garden or a dump? I've heard it said that, scientifically, when we speak, we emit sound waves. These sound waves are carried by atoms and molecules eventually turning into heat energy. With distance and time, the sound waves might fade, but these waves have already spread out and traveled in every direction. The intensity, or energy, with which they are spoken can lengthen the waves' effect on the matter through which it travels. In other words, what you speak will have some kind of physical effect on the things around you. When we think of our words in that way, they take on a whole new level of importance. Science proves what our God's Word has been saying for thousands of years.

> *A wholesome tongue is a tree of life, but perverseness in it breaks the spirit.*
>
> *Pleasant words are like a honeycomb, sweetness to the soul and health to the bones.*
>
> *Death and life are in the power of the tongue, and those who love it will eat its fruit.*
> **—Proverbs 18:21**

Twenty years ago, I became very aware of how I speak. I was given the understanding that if I speak the promises of God's Word about healing to Clemmie, His promises of "plans to prosper you and not to harm you, plans to give you hope and a future" (Jeremiah 29:11 NIV) and "life abundant" (John 10:10) produce joy in Clemmie that, in turn, "does good, like medicine" (Proverbs 17:22). If I speak words of doubt and claim the diagnosis instead of claiming the Healer of the diagnosed issue, I see a "broken spirit which dries the bones" (Proverbs 17:22). I can see with my eyes what God has promised coming to pass when I speak His promises of health and healing instead of bad reports from the doctors. When Clemmie's "soul prospers" (3 John 2), I can physically see his body respond in health, but it starts with a merry heart that trusts the faithfulness of God and His Word. The same goes for all those over whom I speak the life-giving truth of God's Word. "For the word of God is alive and active. Sharper than any double-edged sword, it penetrates even to dividing soul and spirit, joints and marrow; it judges the thoughts and attitudes of the heart" (Hebrews 4:12 NIV).

I see a big difference when I speak blessings and life over my husband and children, as opposed to when I speak words of doubt and bitterness. I am either encouraging and edifying with my words to them, or I am speaking words that are like the "thrusting of a sword," used to destroy and cut deep. Why would I want to do this to anyone, especially to those whom I dearly love? I have found it to be true that family members can be just as destructive with their words as those on the outside of our inner circles. It is easy to take each other for granted and assume that our family members will always forgive and be there for us, even when we behave at our worst. However, our words will either strengthen these relationships or be detrimental to these relationships. Words matter . . . always.

Are we creating something beautiful, or are we destroying something beautiful?

> *And the tongue is a fire, a world of iniquity. The tongue is so set among our members that it defiles the whole body, and sets on fire the course of nature; and it is set on fire by hell. . . . But no man can tame the tongue. It is an unruly evil, full of deadly poison.*
> **—James 3:6, 8**

What do we do if we cannot "tame the tongue"? First of all, we must understand that the tongue is a part of our bodies. How do we present our bodies as a living sacrifice—holy, acceptable to God—which is our spiritual service? Romans 12:1–2 says that in order to do this, we must "renew our minds." We renew our minds through His living and powerful Word. By renewing our minds with His truth, we guard our hearts. Proverbs 4:23–24 tells us to "keep your heart with all diligence, for out of it spring the issues of life. Put away from you a deceitful mouth and put perverse lips far from you." God can and will change our hearts if we renew our minds daily. "I will give you a new heart and put a new spirit within you; I will take the heart of stone out of your flesh and give you a heart of flesh" (Ezekiel 36:26). If we put in truth, we will speak truth. If we fill ourselves up with the world's opinions and deceitful words, we will speak unwholesome words and words of destruction.

There is always evidence of what we put into our heart, by way of our ears and eyes, that comes out of our mouth. "But the things that proceed out of the mouth come forth from the heart, and those things make the man unholy" (Matthew 15:18). I don't know about you, but I do not want to be unholy or create unholy things in my life and the lives of my family members. I would much rather create an Eden than a Sodom. I would prefer to bring forth a tree of life rather than weeds that choke the good seed.

The Passion Translation shares Jesus' words in Matthew 12:35 this way: "When virtue is stored within, the hearts of good, upright people will produce good fruit. But when evil is hidden within, those who are evil will produce evil fruit." What happens to bad, evil fruit? It is eventually cut off and thrown into the fire to be burned. Good fruit will continue to bear more good fruit and give life to everything around it. I can imagine that the once-perfect Garden of Eden was filled with perfectly ripe and tasty fruit that never went bad. I imagine that it was the picture of a beautiful and vibrant array of different flowers and that their fragrance filled the air with a sweet aroma.

This is what God intended when He created it. This is what He expects His people to do with what they speak. "Death and life are in the power of the tongue, and those who love it will eat its fruit" (Proverbs 18:21). Let us not create a trash heap that will only be burned and amount to no good. Let us instead make something beautiful with our words that will bless our children and their children for years to come. "I call heaven and earth as witnesses today against you, that I have set before you life and death, blessing and cursing; therefore choose life, that both you and your descendants may live" (Deuteronomy 30:19). It is our choice to make a beautiful garden or a trash heap. "But I tell you that on the Day of Judgment, men will give account for every careless word they speak" (Matthew 12:36 TLV). Choose wisely.

Revelation: Be careful what you say. Do not speak flippantly. Use every word thoughtfully and purposefully. Speak life to cause it to grow.

PICK UP TRASH OR PICK FLOWERS . . . YOUR CHOICE

WRITE DOWN WHAT THE HOLY SPIRIT SAYS TO YOU:

LESSON 28

"I Messed Up, Mommy! I'm No Good!"

Proverbs 16:3; Ecclesiastes 3:11; Isaiah 60:22; Isaiah 61:3; Jeremiah 17:14; Matthew 19:26; Luke 1:37; Ephesians 3:20; Philippians 4:13; 2 Timothy 4:7–8; Hebrews 4:15

Finishing is better than starting.
Patience is better than pride.
—**Ecclesiastes 7:8** NLT

There is therefore now no condemnation to those who are in Christ Jesus, who do not walk according to the flesh, but according to the Spirit.
—**Romans 8:1**

If you grew up in the eighties, you might know of Bob Ross; perhaps you have even watched some of his painting shows. About five years ago, my youngest took an interest in the reruns of the show, and I found myself once again being lured into watching because of Mr. Ross's soft tones and gentle manner. One of his most famous quotes is: "There are no mistakes, just happy little accidents." In other words, I believe Mr. Ross was saying that any mistake, whether big or small, can be fixed. However, for a nine-year-old perfectionist who thinks he is meant to master every task from the start, that principle is harder to accept.

So, there we were, one hot summer morning. The previous Christmas, Colt had received art supplies from Hobby Lobby after the family had realized his interest in Bob Ross and painting. Our little aspiring artist asked me if he could begin painting his "log cabin in the woods," and of course, I was thrilled to oblige. There, in front of the TV, we set up his easel, canvas, and all the paints Bob Ross had said he needed to paint this "little cabin in the woods." Colt was so excited to get started. As he listened intently to the instructions Mr. Ross gave, I could see his frustration intensifying as his little hands could not keep up. I would pause the program to see if that might help Colt catch up, but the aggravation of not being able to meet his own expectations set in. He put down his brushes, threw up his hands, and exclaimed, "I messed up, Mommy! I'm no good!"

As someone who has battled perfectionism myself, I could empathize with Colt's need to meet his high expectations for himself. It still bothered me greatly when he wanted to give up so quickly. After all, we'd spent money on all those art supplies, and now I had to clean up everything that had been scattered in front of the TV. I strongly encouraged him to come finish what he had started, but to no avail. He reemphasized to me that he could not finish because he had messed up so badly there was no way to make it good. After picking up one of the paintbrushes and dipping it into a little bit of the paint, I began reminding him of Bob Ross's motto—"There are no mistakes, just happy little accidents"—as I began stroking the paintbrush across the areas Colt thought could not be fixed. All it took was a little more paint and a few more brushstrokes for the painting to eventually look a bit more like that "little cabin in the woods." Colt was surprised at the transformation. What he initially thought had no hope for beauty suddenly became a colorful display of patience and persistence, even when the mess-ups seemed irreversible.

If a novice painter like me can take an imperfect painting and make it into something beautiful, or at least into something recognizable, how much more can the Lord of all creation take our mistakes and make them into a beautiful masterpiece for His honor and glory? The Master Artist is ready at all times "to strengthen those crushed by despair who mourn in Zion—to give them a beautiful bouquet in the place of ashes, the oil of bliss instead of tears, and the mantle of joyous praise instead of the spirit of heaviness. Because of this, they will be known as Mighty Oaks of Righteousness, planted by YAHWEH as a living display of His glory" (Isaiah 61:3 TPT). Wow! However, His faithfulness to do this very thing does not give us the excuse to give up when things aren't going the way we expect them to go. Scripture reminds us to press on (Philippians 3:14) in the face of disappointment and discouragement, in Jesus' name. In 2 Timothy 4:7, Paul tells Timothy that he has "fought the good fight, I have finished the race, I have kept the faith." All this did not come without mistakes and adversity. Paul's life was a true example of finishing well, even though his reputation, at least initially, was one stained with the blood of those he once persecuted. The portrait of one who made so many ugly mistakes from not knowing the Savior, Paul was transformed by the power of the Holy Spirit into the most radiant display of God's handiwork.

My prayer is that Colt saw persistence in action, and realized that "all things are possible to him who believes" (Mark 9:23). If you know and trust the God of the impossible, you can press on, knowing that even in our weakness, His strength is revealed (2 Corinthians 12:9). If we do not give up, His promise is true: "He has made everything beautiful in its time. Moreover, He has set eternity in their heart—yet without the possibility that humankind can ever discover the work that God has done from the beginning to the end" (Ecclesiastes 3:11 TLV). I am truly thankful that our Creator never gives up on us or throws us away because of our mistakes and failures. His Master artistry in our lives is unmistakable and perfect. Let Him complete what He started (Philippians 1:6).

"I MESSED UP, MOMMY! I'M NO GOOD!"

Revelation: Do not be discouraged when things are not looking good. Press on! We can do all things through Christ, who strengthens us. Keep painting that picture. The Master Painter will use those brushstrokes to create something beautiful.

FEELS SO GOOD TO LAY DOWN

WRITE DOWN WHAT THE HOLY SPIRIT SAYS TO YOU:

LESSON 29

The Pathway Cleared

Psalm 5:9; Psalm 27:11; Proverbs 2:13; Proverbs 3:5–6;
Proverbs 4:26; Proverbs 15:21; Matthew 3:3; Mark 1:3;
John 1:23; 2 Peter 2:15

You keep in perfect peace one whose mind is stayed on You, because he trusts in You. The way of the righteous is straight. Upright One, You make smooth the path of the righteous.
—Isaiah 26:3, 7 TLV

Make every effort to present yourself before God as tried and true, as an unashamed worker cutting a straight path with the word of truth.
—2 Timothy 2:15 TLV

My oldest son, Clemmie, loves to ride "scooters" (aka four-wheelers). One late spring evening, Clem and I were enjoying our daily ride, him on "Pawpaw's scooter" and me on "Great-Pawpaw's scooter." It was a beautiful evening. My husband had mowed down a beautiful, clear path around the perimeter of the fifty-four-acre hay field. Clem and I begin our ride: him in front, and me following close behind. At first, Clemmie stayed on the clear, "smooth" path that his daddy had mowed especially for Clem to safely ride around the farm.

You see, when the perimeter around the farm is mowed, harmful obstacles become visible. Big rocks and debris can be seen, and even cleared away, before they become hazardous to us on the ATV. When the path is cleared and made smooth, little critters such as rattlesnakes are less likely to stay on that path. Rattlesnakes like to hide in the tall grass instead of being exposed in the short grass. Rattlesnakes, especially, like to take cover among those beautiful Texas bluebonnets and Indian paintbrushes. The taller the grass, the greater the possibility of danger.

Scripture often talks about how our heavenly Father directs our paths. Proverbs 3:5–6 says, "Trust in the LORD with all your heart, and lean not on your own understanding; in all your ways acknowledge Him, and He shall direct your paths." When I look up the Hebrew words for "direct" and "paths" in this verse, I see that the phrase literally means that our God will *make straight, right, pleasant,* and *prosperous* a *well-trodden road* or *highway.* The well-known Psalm 23, specifically verse 3, says, "He leads me in the paths of righteousness for His name's sake." The *Tree of Life Translation* describes the paths of righteousness as "smooth." *Strong's Concordance* translates the Hebrew words in this verse as "He *guides, runs with a sparkle, flows, conducts, protects, sustains, carries, feeds, leads (gently on)* me in the *paths, tracks made right, clear, and cleansed for the purpose of giving* the *name* of Almighty God *honor, authority, fame, and renown.*" Our God has gone before us to clear the way of anything that would cause harm to us, and then He provides everything we need on that path. Why in the world would we want to venture off it and away from His supernatural protection?

Our sin nature and flesh keep us intrigued with the tall grass and the weeds. There is something about being told that we shouldn't do something that makes us want to do that very act. Combined with the thrill of doing something we know we shouldn't, either for the sake of independence or because of utter rebellion, pride is always at the center. Satan utilizes pride, fear, and even beauty when trying to divert our focus off the Savior. Clemmie usually does really well at staying on the mowed path, but every once in a while, he "gets a wild hair" and veers off. You can see him begin to look toward the beautiful and lush bluebonnets. Once he sets his eyes on them, his direction changes. Peter took his eyes off Jesus out of fear of the storm around him. Clem drives off the cleared path because he loves the feeling of independence and is sometimes attracted to the pretty bluebonnets. Whatever the reason, when we take our eyes off of the One who is mighty to save, trouble comes (Zephaniah 3:17; Hebrews 12:2). For in the weeds, and especially in those beautiful lush flowers, the enemy lies ready to strike (Psalm 17:12; 1 Peter 5:8). It doesn't take long for me to remind Clemmie to go back to the cleared path and stay on it. Clemmie knows my voice and trusts that I'm giving him those instructions for his benefit. So, he usually obeys. The Holy Spirit is faithful to do the same for us when we stray from the paths of righteousness. We all need those reminders from time to time. The more we know Him, the more we trust Him, and the more we obey Him.

When Clemmie stays on that pathway that has been mowed for his safety, the dangers of the ride hardly ever affect him. The thistles stay out of the drive train, and the spear grass stays out of the radiator, which keeps the ATV in good shape and decreases the possibility of starting a fire, especially in the hot summer months. The ride is enjoyable and peaceful when we are content to stay on that pathway cleared for our good (Jeremiah 29:11).

THE PATHWAY CLEARED

Revelation: There is joy and peace when we remain in our heavenly Father's protection and provision inside the boundaries our "Daddy" has set for us. We can rejoice and be glad in that truth. Amen.

FEELS SO GOOD TO LAY DOWN

WRITE DOWN WHAT THE HOLY SPIRIT SAYS TO YOU:

LESSON 30

"Put Him Down"

Genesis 22:1–17; Exodus 12; Psalm 127:3–5; Isaiah 53:3–5; Jeremiah 1:5; Romans 12:1–2; 1 Corinthians 6:19–20; Galatians 2:20; Philippians 2:17; 1 Peter 2:5; 1 Peter 4:1–2

> *"'For this child I prayed, and the Lord has granted me my petition which I asked of Him. Therefore I also have lent him to the Lord; as long as he lives he shall be lent to the Lord.' So they worshiped the Lord there."*
> **—1 Samuel 1:27–28**

> *"Do not store up for yourselves treasures on earth, where moths and vermin destroy, and where thieves break in and steal. But store up for yourselves treasures in heaven, where moths and vermin do not destroy, and where thieves do not break in and steal. For where your treasure is, there your heart will be also."*
> **—Matthew 6:19–20** NIV

It was April 22, 2004, when we received the diagnosis of a "rare genetic disorder" for our firstborn son, Clemmie. Clem was around seven and a half months old, and we had just finished our assignment at Travis Air Force Base, California. We were living in a small apartment in San Antonio, Texas, while Shad was in training to be an instructor pilot at Laughlin Air Force Base, a pilot training base in Del Rio, Texas. What was supposed to only be a three-month TDY in San Antonio turned into five months. We were also being reassigned back to Enid, Oklahoma, and Vance Air Force Base, since it was closer to a large children's hospital. It was the most heartbreaking time of our lives. It also brought about the biggest spiritual awakening of our lives as we were desperate for comfort and answers from the Holy Spirit more than we'd ever been before.

I remember sitting in the dark room rocking Clemmie in his nursery. I was weeping . . . *really* weeping for my son. I was crying out to the Lord for answers. I did not ask Him, "Why?" in this particular conversation. That question had been asked a couple of days before, and the Lord had responded to me in my spirit with, *When did sickness enter this world?* I answered, *Sickness entered when sin entered.* His response was, *Did I not take all of sin and its punishment on the cross?* I knew then that I wanted to dig deep into His Word and promises. I would learn so much during those five months as He taught me His will through Scripture.

"PUT HIM DOWN"

It was in this dark room, however, while rocking my precious son, that the Holy Spirit would do a *new thing* in my life. Clemmie had been difficult to put down in his crib without him waking up and crying for me to come pick him back up again. The slightest movement away from the comfort of Mommy's warm body would cause Clem to awaken in distress. We now know why, as he was having "complex-partial" seizures multiple times a day, every day. That specific night, between rocking and weeping, I would stealthily try to lay Clemmie down to sleep in his crib. Each time, he would wake up crying for me to pick him up again. I was tired, and I was weary. It was not only literally dark in the nursery that night, but it was a very dark time in our lives, and I was craving direction from my God. I was *desperate* to hear what He had to say. As I wept and prayed, asking for help, an audible voice suddenly said, "Put him down." I was startled! I looked around the dark room to see if Shad had possibly come in without me knowing. He had not. In a split second, a battle began to take place in my mind. Satan began telling me that if I were to put Clem down at that moment, he would wake up, and I would have to start all over again. Again, I heard the same voice, this time in my spirit, saying, "Put him down." It startled me so much that I just froze, and again, the devil reminded me that Clem would wake up if I put him down. Then, a third time, the Holy Spirit told me to "Put him down." This time I got up and laid Clemmie in his crib. As Clem lay there, sound asleep, I felt a peace that I hadn't felt since before the diagnosis. This peace was different, though. It wasn't a peace I had because everything was going right and there was no trouble. Instead, it was a complete peace right smack-dab in the midst of sorrow. It was then that I began to understand "the peace of God, which surpasses all understanding" (Philippians 4:7). I experience *quietness* and *rest*, fully confident in "the LORD that heals" (Exodus 15:26).

As I left that dark room where Clemmie was sound asleep, I walked over to Shad, who was studying at the foot of the bed. He must've seen that I had been crying. He looked at me with tenderness, fully understanding why my eyes were puffy and red. I told him what had happened, and we both came to the realization that the Lord was simply telling us to give our son back to Him. He would meet His needs. He would heal. He would save. He would be faithful, and we could rest in that.

That night I went to bed in "perfect peace" (Isaiah 26:3) because I had heard the voice of the Lord, and I knew that when I put Clemmie down that night, I had also offered him back to the Lord, just as Hannah had done with Samuel in 1 Samuel 1:27–28. I also feel as if I had just laid him down at the foot of the cross, where Jesus, with arms stretched wide, had Clem's name written on every stripe He bore, and by those stripes, Clem was being made *whole* (Isaiah 53:5). He was, and still is, the Savior and Healer, and I was not going to stand in the way of the Master creating a beautiful masterpiece from what the world would say was a hopeless, disordered human being. "For God is not a God

"PUT HIM DOWN"

of disorder but of peace—as in all the congregations of the Lord's people" (1 Corinthians 14:33 NIV). Over the next five months, the Holy Spirit would continue to confirm His will for Clemmie, and our hearts would begin to mend. That dark night, I laid Clem on the altar, and our faithful heavenly Father showed us that He had already provided the Lamb in Clemmie's place (Genesis 22:1–17; John 1:29). It was now up to us to believe and receive *all* (Exodus 12:5–10) of that perfect, complete sacrifice on behalf of our son, then walk in the complete victory He gave us at the cross. Our prayer and commitment since that time has been Psalm 103:1–5: "Bless the LORD, O my soul; and all that is within me, bless His holy name! Bless the LORD, O my soul, and forget not all His benefits: who forgives all your iniquities, who heals all your diseases, who redeems your life from destruction, who crowns you with lovingkindness and tender mercies, who satisfies your mouth with good things, so that your youth is renewed like the eagle's."

Twenty years later, our Lord continues to confirm His Word. We have seen it active in Clemmie's life (Hebrews 4:12). In fact, Clemmie loves the Word of God. It is medicine to Clem and "health to all [his] flesh" (Proverbs 4:22). Yes, the battle against the enemy, who comes to "steal, and to kill, and to destroy" (John 10:10) is fierce at times, and we have grown weary, but His Word is where we place our confidence. We "walk by faith, not by sight" (2 Corinthians 5:7).

It has not been easy or popular to have this kind of

faith. We have been discouraged and scolded a few times for believing that Jesus' broken body had anything to do with our physical healing. I could write a whole book on that. The Scriptures from Genesis to Revelation confirms that His desire and will is for His people to be well. Precept upon precept, His Word, and His character, proves it: "I would have lost heart, unless I had believed that I would see the goodness of the LORD in the land of the living" (Psalm 27:13). We trust that our God is faithful to do as He has promised. We must believe it! Over these twenty years, we've seen glimpses of Clemmie's healing, and although his testimony is still unfolding, we are confident that "He who began a good work in [Clem] will perfect it until the day of Christ Jesus" (Philippians 1:6 NASB). He will do the same for you. Praise the Lord!

Revelation: Give everything to Jesus, especially your children. Do not hold on to them as if they are an earthly treasure. They are His, first. Let Him do His work in them and show His glory!

"PUT HIM DOWN"

WRITE DOWN WHAT THE HOLY SPIRIT SAYS TO YOU:

LESSON 31

"Life Is Like a Popcorn Toot"

Psalm 39:4–6, 11; Psalm 103:15–16; Ecclesiastes 6:12; Ecclesiastes 12:6–7; Job 14:1–15

Behold, you have made my days a few handbreadths, and my lifetime is as nothing before you. Surely all mankind stands as a mere breath!
—Psalm 39:5 ESV

Yet you do not know what your life will be like tomorrow. What is your life? For you are a vapor that appears for a little while and then vanishes.
—James 4:14

I have been married to my husband for almost twenty-seven years now, and I am still caught off-guard, and become a little tickled, when he quotes Scripture in "Texan." He could probably write a biblical translation that all Texans could relate to and understand. There would be KJV, NIV, NKJV, NLT, TLV, EVS, and "Translated Texan Version" (TTV).

One morning Shad and I sat together at our kitchen island discussing how to counsel someone who confessed to giving in to fleshly desires. We do some of our best problem-solving, praying, and deep theology at our kitchen island. Our conversation quickly turned to how life is too short to make the same bad choices continually. So many of us choose to live life committing the same sins, and then we wonder why things never get better. We make excuses to defend those sins, even counting them as *small* or nonconsequential. We believe what is done in secret will not be discovered. We continue in our sin because we believe it makes us happy. Our lives become an endless merry-go-round of hurtful consequences that keep us on an emotional high one moment and in the depths of despair the next. "So what do we do, then? Do we persist in sin so that God's kindness and grace will increase? What a terrible thought! We have died to sin once and for all, as a dead man passes away from this life. So how could we live under sin's rule a moment longer?" (Romans 6:1–2 TPT). When we truly understand that *life is like a popcorn toot*, and each moment is a fleeting vapor, why would we want to waste any moment sinning?

Through the inspiration of the Holy Spirit, Paul tells us

in Hebrews, "For if we keep on sinning willfully after we have received the knowledge of the truth, there no longer remains a sacrifice for sins, but only terrifying expectation of judgment and a fury of fire about to devour the enemies of God" (Hebrews 10:26–27 TLV). That sounds pretty serious to me. So, why continue to do the wrong things? First John 3:6 says, "No one who abides in Him keeps on sinning; no one who sins has seen Him or known Him." The simple answer to the "why" is that we do not really *abide* with the Savior of the world. We do not make the time to *stay, continue, dwell, endure, be present,* and *remain* in His presence. It is when we *abide* with Him that His character becomes our character. When a son spends lots of time with his daddy, does he not reflect his dad's character? Does a daughter not know the depths of her daddy's love when she spends time with him? How much more would we know and understand our heavenly Father by spending time with Him in prayer and in His Word? We would learn so much if we would be still in His presence and listen to Him speak (Psalm 46:10).

I don't know if it is because of my age or because we are getting news faster about people dying, but I am reminded daily of how short our life here on earth is compared to eternity. When we compare everything with eternity, we see the urgency in telling people about Jesus. We understand how important it is not to be a slave to sin anymore. Time must be used effectively to be witnesses (Acts 1:8) and "ministers of the new covenant" (2 Corinthians 3:6).

Psalm 39:4–5 in the *New Living Translation* says, "Lord, remind me how brief my time on earth will be. Remind me that my days are numbered—how fleeting my life is. You have made my life no longer than the width of my hand. My entire lifetime is just a moment to you; at best, each of us is but a breath," or *popcorn toot!* Our lives last only a short moment in the timeline of eternity. So, why let our lives be known by sin instead of known for the One who saved us from sin?

If we honestly want to make the most out of each moment the Lord gives us, we will do as James tells us: "So then, surrender to God. Stand up to the devil and resist him and he will flee in agony. Move your heart closer and closer to God, and he will come even closer to you. But make sure you cleanse your life, you sinners, and keep your heart pure and stop doubting. Feel the pain of your sin, be sorrowful and weep! Let your joking around be turned into mourning and your joy into deep humiliation. Be willing to be made low before the Lord and he will exalt you!" (James 4:7–10 tpt). When is the last time we felt the pain of our sin? When we truly feel the horrible sting of our sin, and we humble ourselves, He will then be the "lifter of [our] head" (Psalm 3:3 esv). Lastly, remember Psalm 119:11, which is one of the first verses I memorized at a young age: "Your word I have hidden in my heart, that I might not sin against You."

May that be our goal and our prayer every moment of every day we are given.

Revelation: Our life on this earth is too short not to live completely surrendered to our Savior. If we live with the understanding of His sacrifice to keep us out of sin, we will live in that freedom and not be a slave to sin any longer.

WRITE DOWN WHAT THE HOLY SPIRIT SAYS TO YOU:

LESSON 32

Preparing the Soil

Leviticus 26:5; Isaiah 17:10–11; Hosea 6:1–2, 11; Mark 4; John 4:36; James 3:18; 2 Timothy 2:6

Those who sow in tears will reap with a song of joy. Whoever keeps going out weeping, carrying his bag of seed, will surely come back with a song of joy, carrying his sheaves.
—Psalm 126:5–6 TLV

Those too lazy to plow in the right season will have no food at the harvest.
—Proverbs 20:4 NLT

So then neither he who plants is anything, nor he who waters, but God who gives the increase. Now he who plants and he who waters are one, and each one will receive his own reward according to his own labor. For we are God's fellow workers; you are God's field, you are God's building.
—1 Corinthians 3:7–9

Shad and I met in the summer of 1994. After a two-year friendship, we began dating in the fall of 1996. We knew each other pretty well because of our friendship. I understood that his heart's desire was to fly airplanes and eventually live on a farm with lots of land somewhere in the great state of Texas, where he was born and raised. He loved the smell of jet fuel, but the smell of freshly plowed soil was even more exhilarating for him. Within three weeks after we married in December 1997, we were sent away from Texas to serve our country in the United States Air Force. Wherever the Air Force told us to go, there was always a longing to come back home after retirement from the military.

Retirement finally came in May 2017, and we were excited to be moving back to Texas. In fact, we bought the farm directly across the field from Shad's parents' farm, where he was raised. It was without any shadow of a doubt God-ordained, but we had no idea of the amount of work that would be needed in "preparing the soil" for harvest in every area of our lives.

A little over twenty years of living away had given us a deep appreciation for being close to loved ones again. As with most moves back home, things were different. Shad's daddy had gone home to be with Jesus in September 2016, just seven and a half months before Shad's retirement. We had big dreams of living close to "PawPaw" Bill, but those dreams of him riding four-wheelers with the boys, teaching them how to fix things, and watching them grow would not

PREPARING THE SOIL

come to fruition. I imagine he would have loved helping us make our new place a home, and he and Shad would've embraced the time together rebuilding and restoring what was old and worn into something new and beautiful. We have definitely missed that.

Our first year on the farm was spent working on the house and the forty acres. The pasture had great potential, but undesirable elements were beginning to take control. We needed to rehabilitate the soil to be productive and fertile. Shad was up for the task. I had no idea of the amount of work it was going to take, but I was about to learn.

Our goal was to first *rid* the pasture of a number of mesquite tree saplings. If you know anything about mesquite trees, you know they are highly invasive, thorny, and very difficult to kill. A mesquite tree will choke out any other vegetation around it. These thorny trees were popping up throughout the pasture and needed immediate attention. The larger mesquite trees grow, the more difficult they are to kill. Therefore, we needed to get them while they were small. After carefully examining the land, we identified them, tagged them with orange ribbon, and sprayed them with special herbicide. One would think that would suffice to eradicate them, but not with these tenacious timbers. After allowing the herbicide time to work, which took about two weeks, we needed to hire someone to come in with a "grubber" to dig out the root ball. The *root* must be *completely taken out*. Leaving the smallest remnants of the tree will allow the brush to return with a vengeance.

According to Shad, the battle to eradicate the mesquites, like grass burrs, never ends. We must stay vigilant to target and exterminate as we discover them. Even seven years later, we continue to examine the land for any sign of them. If we get complacent and think all is well, they will come back.

After removing the mesquite saplings, it was time to mow the pasture down to the dirt so we could then pick up big and small rocks that were scattered everywhere. It took several hours to *shred*, and it took several days to *pick up rocks* on the forty acres. The *removal of rocks* would be an important step in helping the new sprigs we were going to plant to take root and stay alive.

After the mesquites and big rocks were gone, and the pasture was cleared, it was time to *plow* the dirt. We plowed the pasture every four weeks for a full year. *Plowing*, or *turning the soil*, not only helps to *prevent weeds* from growing, but it *stirs up nutrients* in the soil. Plowing also *mellows* the soil, *breaking up hard clods* of dirt and *allowing for deeper root growth*. The more we plow, the more malleable the soil, the better the bed for the new sprigs. Could any of this soil preparation be analogous to our spiritual growth and walk with the Lord? I was now experiencing the beginnings of what it meant to be a farm girl. I was also beginning to better understand the Scriptures about the *soil*, the *seed*, and the *Sower*.

After a full year of plowing each month, the field

was now ready to receive the seed. It was time to begin planting, but the day of planting needed to meet certain weather conditions. Of course, a rainy day would not have been an ideal time to plant. Also, we needed it to be a fairly calm day with little wind. That is rare at our place. You see, our farm is on a hill so there is always a strong breeze. If the day of planting had sixty-mile-per-hour winds, some of the sprigs would've been carried away and not gone into the ground. The sprigs might have instead scattered and fallen on the highway in front of our place. They would have wasted.

The Lord provided the perfect day for sprigging. We hired a husband-and-wife team with a "sprigger" to place the new sprigs in the ground. Once the sprigs were in the ground, we gave the sprigs a full year to take root and grow. Our prayer was that, with all the preparation of the soil, the grass would grow well and produce a great harvest. Our great God again provided the rain and sunshine needed to give growth. He is so faithful!

It was on the *third* year that we were finally able to reap the harvest. It took *three years* to cleanse the field, till the soil, plant the seed, and watch the seed grow before we experienced a *complete* harvest. In a later lesson, we will find out why the number *three* is so important. Friends, nothing happens by chance or coincidence. Almighty God is very thoughtful in how and when He provides. If we had not prepared the soil properly, and if the seed had not had the proper amount of rain and sunshine, would the seed have taken root and grown? Most likely not.

In the gospels of Matthew, Mark, and Luke, Jesus preached to the multitudes giving a parable about the *soil*, the *seed*, and the *Sower*. Let's look, first, at Matthew's account of Jesus' warning about the seed that "fell by the *wayside*; and the birds came and devoured them" (Matthew 13:4). Now look at how Mark described Jesus' teaching about the seed falling on *rocky ground*: "Other seed fell on shallow soil with underlying rock. The seed sprouted quickly because the soil was shallow. But the plant soon wilted under the hot sun, and since it didn't have deep roots, it died" (Mark 4:5–6 NLT). Jesus also warned against the *soil with thorns*: "Other seed fell among the thorns; and the thorns grew and choked it, and it yielded no crop" (Mark 4:7 TLV). Finally, He spoke of the *good soil*: "Still other seed fell on good soil. It came up and yielded a crop, a hundred times more than was sown" (Luke 8:8 NIV).

When the disciples asked Him the meaning of the parable, His response was this, in Luke 8:11–15: "The seed is the word of God. Those by the wayside are the ones who hear; then the devil comes and takes away the word out of their hearts, lest they should believe and be saved" (Luke 8:11–12). The "wayside" on the Vinson Farm would be the *highway* that runs alongside the front of our pasture. If extra seed or sprigs were to fall along this highway, they would land on asphalt. Any sprig would quickly dry up and die on the hot asphalt. There would also be no way for it to take root and grow on that hard surface. Also, the birds would definitely take it and eat it.

Jesus goes on to explain about the seed, or the Word of God, that fell on "rocky soil" in Mark 4:16–17 (NLT): "The seed on the rocky soil represents those who hear the message and immediately receive it with joy. But since they don't have deep roots, they don't last long. They fall away as soon as they have problems or are persecuted for believing God's word." If Shad and I would have let those big rocks stay in our pasture, sure, some grass might have *appeared* to be growing among the rocks. However, the heat of the Texas sun would quickly scorch the shallow grass, or a big storm would come with its sixty-mile-per-hour winds and heavy rain. That grass would be washed up and blown away. Not only that, but those big rocks would've caused problems for the plow and the softening of the soil.

Mark's account of Jesus' words regarding the *soil with thorns* is this: "And others are the ones sown among the thorns. They have heard the word; but the worries of the world, the seduction of wealth, and the desires for other things enter in and choke the word, and it becomes unfruitful" (Mark 4:18–19 TLV). I have witnessed how those thorny mesquite trees can take over a field rapidly and leave little space for the good grass to grow. What do you do with a field of thorny bushes? How productive and beneficial would a pasture of thorny bushes really be? Any good growth would be choked out and taken over by those thorny trees.

Jesus ends the Parable of the Sower with this: "But the seed on good soil stands for those with a noble and good heart, who hear the word, retain it, and by persevering produce a crop" (Luke 8:15 NIV). I would like to think we now have good soil here on the Vinson Farm. It took a lot of work to remove the thorns, take out the rocks, and clean the pasture. It took time to plow and turn the soil over and over to create a good environment for the seed to take root and grow. It takes us being vigilant to maintain the area and stay on the lookout for mesquite saplings and rocks that have surfaced. In order for the ground to be *fruitful*, we must *persevere* in the work to maintain *good soil*.

The question for all of us should be this: *What kind of soil am I for the Sower?* Our God wants His Word to be *planted deep* in our hearts so that we would produce the *fruit of righteousness* (Philippians 1:11; Hebrews 12:11; James 3:18). Is the Word of God planted deeply in us—so deeply that we can recall it, pray it, speak it over our circumstances, and live it out for the world to see? Or is the Word of God only on the surface, in word only but not in deed? Are we quick to give up on God's promises because things aren't going our way? Do the trials of this life cause us to doubt the faithfulness of God? Are we willing to persevere through all the plowing of the soil of our lives so that God can make us good soil? *Lord, eradicate the thorns and dig out their roots. Pick up the rocks and work the soil of our lives so that it becomes soft and fertile for Your Word to flourish and grow in us, in Jesus' name.*

Revelation: The Holy Spirit will do the work to make the soil of our lives ready to receive seed from the Sower, who is almighty God. We need to surrender and truly allow Him time to restore the field back to new life through Jesus Christ.

FEELS SO GOOD TO LAY DOWN

WRITE DOWN WHAT THE HOLY SPIRIT SAYS TO YOU:

LESSON 33

He Does More

Matthew 13:57; Matthew 10:14; Mark 6:1–6;
Galatians 6:9; Revelation 3:1–6; Revelation 3:14–22

"'For My thoughts are not your thoughts, nor are your ways My ways.' It is a declaration of ADONAI. 'For as the heavens are higher than earth, so are My ways higher than your ways, and My thoughts than your thoughts.'"
—Isaiah 55:8–9 TLV

So let us not lose heart in doing good, for in due time we will reap if we don't give up. Therefore, whenever we have an opportunity, let us do good toward all—especially those who belong to the household of faith.
—Galatians 6:9–10 TLV

It has been seven years since we moved from Maryland to this small town. My husband spent his entire childhood and through his early college years here. So, we came back to where he grew up. This is the town where my mother-in-law, now a widow, still lives. "But if a widow has children or grandchildren, these should learn first of all to put their religion into practice by caring for their own family and so repaying their parents and grandparents, for this is pleasing to God" (1 Timothy 5:4 NIV). We believed, in obedience to God, that we were to live near my mother-in-law and honor her.

I am so very thankful for how the Lord provided this farm just across the field from my husband's parents' farm, where he grew up, but there have been obstacles to overcome. The couple who owned this place for twenty-five years had been holding it for us for when we retired from the Air Force. They held it for ten years after we had originally planned to separate from the military, but when their health eventually prevented them from taking care of the place, they needed to sell and move closer to their own children in North Texas. It was our God's perfect timing that we retired at the same time they had to sell and move. So, we bought the farm.

Although we'd made many small visits to this town in our first twenty years of marriage, I was still relatively unknown to many here. However, everybody remembers the little blond-haired, blue-eyed boy who grew up in this town. I am simply that little boy's wife. I've heard story after story of Shad's growing-up years and the different memories each one has of my husband. It really has been fun listening to all of the stories, and it has given me greater insight into how my husband grew up and what helped make him the man he is today. That has been one of the beautiful things about coming back home.

I am also grateful to now live so close to family. After living hundreds of miles away for twenty years, it has been wonderful to drive only a couple of hours up the highway to spend quality time with my parents, sisters, and their families. It has been such a blessing to gather at our house for birthdays and holidays. I've loved it! The small hike across the field to MawMaw's house is also simply wonderful, although we greatly miss the man who shared our vision of coming back home and buying this farm. Shad's daddy went home to live forever with the One he proclaimed as Savior and Lord seven and a half months before Shad retired, eleven months before we bought the farm, and eleven months and one day before Shad became an employee for the same company his dad had worked for, for over thirty-five years. This was another dream that became reality, all in God's perfect timing. I know Bill would have been so involved with helping us bring to life a beautiful homestead for his grandsons, and I look forward to seeing him again really soon. Come, Lord Jesus (Revelation 22:20)!

Though we had several opportunities to sing in more

places across the United States *because* of our time in the military, the music ministry with my sisters had slowed down. This change of pace in our ministry gave us time to start our own families and be present for our husbands and our children. The three of us also served our local churches faithfully in music ministry. Our Lord was equipping us as individuals to edify our own local church bodies. Specifically, I had been used to prepare the music for worship services, lead worship, and direct the choirs and orchestras in each of the different churches where we were members—from California to Oklahoma to Maryland. We never stopped serving the Lord in music right where He placed us. It was really a time of growth for all three of us.

However, I was always preparing for the time when the Haynes Sisters would continue our ministry together. Tonya and Tara waited patiently as I served my country as the wife of a military man, making a home for him to come back to from every assignment and every mission he was given in his twenty years of active-duty service. It was so important that I was there for my husband. "'Entreat me not to leave you, or to turn back from following after you; for wherever you go, I will go; and wherever you lodge, I will lodge; your people shall be my people, and your God, my God'" (Ruth 1:16). I've seen the effects on our military men and women coming home to a "Dear John" letter from spouses who could not handle the military life, but the covenant I made commissioned me to stand firm with my covenant partner, to go where he goes, and to continue to commit even when it gets hard. We remained faithful to that covenant.

After our move back to Texas, we began looking for a local church body where we could be in fellowship and use our gifts to edify the body of believers. We followed my father-in-law's wise counsel to look for a church that would provide for our specific needs in music ministry and in a great special needs ministry for Clem. We visited, and we even became involved in those ministries, at a large church in the Waco area. It was good, but the overwhelming desire to minister to the small community in which we actually lived, and where our boys went to school, kept us from becoming completely content with that church.

After I finally met with the worship pastor and explaining how the Holy Spirit was leading us to serve in the local church closer to where we lived, he prayed with me, gave his blessing, and understood the call. We then invited the pastor of our small-town church, and his wife, over for supper. We've purposed to do this at every local church we intended to join so that we could discuss the vision of the church and share our hearts for both music and special needs ministry. After having the pastor and his wife over for supper and talking about how we could help edify and serve our local church, we made the decision to join the church in which my husband had grown up. We knew it wasn't going to be easy, but we also knew the Lord had placed us in this town "for such a time as this" (Esther 4:14). We poured every ounce of our time, talents, and resources into it. We taught Sunday school. We organized a designated room for our special needs kids. I also helped introduce new songs to the congregation and led worship when the song leader was gone. I was directing the children's choir, and I was looking forward to helping grow an adult choir to help lead worship on Sunday mornings. It seemed that exciting things were happening. We listened to the renewed hopes of many in the church who had been longing for an active music ministry, a children's ministry, a women's ministry, a thriving adults Sunday school class for those younger than sixty, and, yes, even an organized special needs ministry. We came to find out that there were others in the community looking for a smaller church with a ministry for their child with special needs. At the time we were there, three teenagers were hoping we could meet this specific need in their lives. The Lord was ready to work through this ministry, but was the church ready to plant the seed and see it grow? "The point is this: whoever sows sparingly shall also reap sparingly, and whoever sows bountifully shall also reap bountifully" (2 Corinthians 9:6 TLV).

Over the next two years, however, we encountered increased resistance, which was only exacerbated by COVID. It became more evident that change and moving beyond traditions was not wanted, at least not at that tim. Maintaining the status quo seemed to be the preferred course. After much prayer, we were led to seek other places to serve (Matthew 10:14 TLV).

It was a very lonely and isolated time for us, but in God's perfect timing, He opened another door. I received a call from a local pastor who had been praying about starting a new worship service in town. People were not satisfied with "church as usual," and some were hungry for change. Coming out of the seclusion of the COVID lockdowns, with new folks moving into the area, an opportunity to do something *new* was revealed, and we wanted to be a part of that! Isaiah 43:19 (TLV) says, "Here I am, doing a new thing; now it is springing up—do you not know about it? I will surely make a way in the desert, rivers in the wasteland." Refuge Worship began meeting on Sunday nights, and young people seemed excited at first. However, the numbers soon began to dwindle. To address this, we changed from meeting on Sunday nights to Saturday nights, which seemed to bring in a different crowd. It was a small group to be sure, but it was one that was committed. Although Refuge never really took off like we had hoped or imagined, we remained faithful to worship together for two years. Refuge was a worship service where those who might not necessarily have felt welcomed in the other churches came to worship in freedom. Needless to say, we were not the traditional church crowd. We were a congregation of people coming from multiple denominations and backgrounds. The Lord even brought in a group of special needs adults who loved worshiping with us. They were actively participating in worship, and they were faithful.

Though we only met with Refuge for two years, it was an open door for new ministries to be planted in the town. Through a vision, the Holy Spirit led us to start a "Holy Hayride" on our farm during harvest season. This ministry continues to grow and be an avenue for the Gospel of Jesus Christ to be shared with people in the community and beyond.

Additionally, partnering with the local pastors, we instituted "Community Christmas." This musical event, which includes a choir, instrumentalists, and actors, is held downtown and is made up of members from many local churches in the community and beyond. The first year, approximately three hundred people attended, out of a population of around 1,500. The second year, it was exceedingly cold outside, but we still had close to two hundred in attendance. In the third year, attendance was back up to over three hundred people. Now in our fourth year of "Community Christmas," we see people excited to be a part of something bigger than themselves, an event that brings all the local churches together to proclaim the Good News of Jesus Christ in word and in song.

As a result of all these new opportunities in the last seven years, I've developed friendships with other like-minded people, specifically women from the different churches in town. I am seeing the results of many prayers for revival and a fresh outpouring of the Spirit begin to unfold through repentance, healing, and restoration. I believe this is the way *the* Church was originally designed by God to be. I am not alone in this small town. I have been told these women have been praying for a mighty move of the Holy Spirit for years. They have been steadfast and not quit just because they did not see it happening right away. I am so encouraged by these warriors for Jesus.

Never cease praying and praising our heavenly Father for His will to be done "on earth as it is in heaven" (Matthew 6:10). Don't give up! In these *last* of the last days, the Church cannot simply be a place where we sing together and listen to a good sermon. We *must* be a place where people meet with a supernatural God who calls us to repentance, restores, heals, justifies, and sanctifies *all* those who come. *That* is how we will reach a lost world. May His Spirit set a fire in us to pursue what He has called us to do passionately, in Jesus' name!

I love this small town, and I will always be devoted to seeing its people prosper just as their souls prosper (3 John 1:2). May we be a people not complacent, but passionate about growing future generations to love and serve the Most High with all their heart, soul, mind, and strength.

May we be compassionate for the lost so that they may be found. May revival start here and now, and may it begin with me, in this small town. Do even more, Lord!

Revelation: Recognize the people and opportunities the Lord brings your way. It might not appear as expected. He exceeds our expectations when we remain faithful. Do not lose heart, and don't give up on people. Though doors may close, always look for the Lord to open new doors. Serve Him where He needs you.

HE DOES MORE

WRITE DOWN WHAT THE HOLY SPIRIT SAYS TO YOU:

LESSON 34

"Don't Drop the Fruit"

Ezekiel 47:12; Proverbs 11:30; Proverbs 31:31; Isaiah 11:2; Matthew 7:16–18; John 15; Romans 8:9; Romans 8:16; Galatians 5:17; Ephesians 5:9; Colossians 3:12; 2 Peter 1:5–8; James 1:19

"And I will rebuke the devourer for your sakes, so that he will not destroy the fruit of your ground, nor shall the vine fail to bear fruit for you in the field," says the Lord of hosts.

—Malachi 3:11

But the fruit produced by the Holy Spirit within you is divine love in all its varied expressions: joy that overflows, peace that subdues, patience that endures, kindness in action, a life full of virtue, faith that prevails, gentleness of heart, and strength of spirit. Never set the law above these qualities, for they are meant to be limitless.

—Galatians 5:22–23 TPT

I have been a student of music my whole life. From the time I was in the womb, I was listening to my dad, a minister of music and youth, direct choirs and lead people into worship through music. As a toddler, I was watching and hearing the same at choir rehearsals, worship services, and youth retreats. My first experience singing in an organized choir was under my mom's leadership, and my first solo, "Jesus, I Heard You Had a Big House," took place when I was four years old. My sisters and I started making harmony together soon after that first solo, and we continue that ministry, even today. Music was what I loved and where I thrived. I studied it, I memorized it, I lived it. I believe God gave knitted a song in my heart when He formed me in the womb, and I was to declare that song all my life.

So, I dedicated my time to music, choirs and orchestras instead of playing sports. I really liked sports, though, and I am actually very competitive. I enjoyed playing kickball with my sisters, cousins, uncles, and PawPaw. I enjoyed throwing the football with boys in the youth group. I enjoyed my short time on the tennis team. I might've been a good athlete, but I devoted my time and energy to nurturing the musical talents God had given me.

After moving to California, where we had our first military assignment out of pilot training, Shad and I found ourselves needing community. The very first place we found it was in the two KC-10 squadrons. Together, that group became like family. Our husbands would deploy, and we would check on each other, and get together, to keep up morale. The base also had team sports that each squadron and their spouses could join. Shad and I joined the squadron's softball teams. Shad's team was made up of the men from the two squadrons, and my team, "The Gucci Gals," was made up of women from the two squadrons. Most of the ladies were wives, but we did have a few female pilots who joined in on the fun. I always looked forward to our practices and games, especially when our husbands were gone for months at a time. I built strong relationships with these ladies. These military wives are some of the strongest women I know. There was nothing they could not endure and handle by themselves. They were the ones to keep the home front intact and well-organized in preparation for their husbands' return. However, we needed each other, and we understood the importance of strengthening our relationships.

One such instance of understanding our need for each other came as we were playing a softball game against the Security Forces squadron. These ladies were serious softball players, and their coach was just as serious about winning the game. It was my time up to bat. Just as the ball came across home plate, I swung. *Smack!* It was a base hit. My competitive juices were flowing as I stood on first base. I was nervous but pretty confident that the batter after me would get me to second base. She not only got me to second base, but she hit that ball so hard I was able to take second, then third, and then I was directed home. My team was so excited. As I ran from home plate over to the dugout, through the cheers of my teammates I heard my coach yell, "Tiffany, they don't believe you touched home plate!" Without any hesitation, I ran back to home plate and stomped on the plate with extreme fervor. As I stomped, I stared right at the Security Forces coach, then said, "There! Is that good enough for you?" With head held high and a haughty spirit, I jogged back to the dugout. There, I was met with plenty of high-fives and "atta-girl" pats on the back. I was really something. Little did I know that I was about to be humbled. Second Samuel 22:28 says, "You save lowly people. But Your eyes are on the haughty—You will humble them." As I went to sit down on the bench in the dugout, one of the other wives was quietly waiting there for me. I thought she was going to congratulate me like all my other teammates had done, but instead she looked at me intently, and with love in her eyes and a gentle smile, she said, "Don't drop the fruit." At that moment all the air in my inflated ego was sucked out. She was right! I immediately knew what she meant. I had just dropped the fruit of the Holy Spirit in me. I knew her to be a firmly grounded and committed sister in Christ, so because these wise words of admonishment came from someone who had a genuine reputation of godliness (Romans 15:14), I received her gentle correction. I began to apologize to her and all my teammates in the dugout. After the game, I apologized for my extreme behavior to the opposing team's coach as well. As far as everyone was concerned, everything was all good.

"DON'T DROP THE FRUIT"

However, these ladies, especially the commander's wife, will always remember the time when Tiffany lost control. No matter how much I apologized in sincerity, the memory of my anger and pride will still be the most vivid in their minds. Most of them thought it was a well-deserved act of defiance and competitiveness against a team who was clearly being just as competitive and defamatory in their treatment of us. However, I have been called to be different and set apart from those who do not have the Spirit of the Living God within them. I had dropped the fruit of *love* for others, *joy* in adversity, *peace* in the midst of aggravation, *patience* toward those who accused, *kindness* to those in opposition, *goodness* and virtue for the sake of revenge, *faithfulness* to show others Jesus, *gentleness* just to show *my own* strength, and *self-control* in order to prove I was right. How much did this one moment affect others coming to know Jesus as their personal Savior and Lord? I didn't just drop the fruit. I slung the whole basket!

If we were to think about the consequences of our actions before we act, we would do well. I have been reminded of this moment many times in my life. Ecclesiastes 7:5 (TLV) says, "Better to hear a rebuke from the wise than to listen to the song of fools." The words, "Don't drop the fruit," spoken by my wise sister in Christ were the admonishment I needed to remind me to demonstrate the fruit of the Holy Spirit and not the flesh. It would have been very easy for me to ignore her rebuke and bask in the laughter and cheers from my other teammates. "May it never be! How can we who died to sin still live in it?" (Romans 6:2 TLV). Am I faithfully producing the fruit of His righteousness moment by moment without making excuses for an unfruitful life? First Peter 2:16 (NIV) says, "Live as free people, but do not use your freedom as a cover-up for evil; live as God's slaves."

Realize this also, that just because people have leaves doesn't mean they bear fruit (John 15:2). I was reminded of this when listening to a sermon on Palm Sunday. The same people who waved those *leafy* palm branches and said, "Hosanna to the Son of David! Blessed is He who comes in the name of the LORD!" (Matthew 21:9) are the same people who days later yelled, "Crucify Him!" (Matthew 27:20–23 NIV). Do we say we follow Him yet deny Him with our actions? May it never be, in Jesus' name. Let us draw in close to Him, know Him more through His Word and Spirit, and allow Him to produce the *fruit* in our lives so that others will want to know Him. "The fruit of righteousness is a tree of life, and he who wins souls is wise" (Proverbs 11:30). We win souls by exhibiting His righteous fruit, so may we never "drop the fruit."

"DON'T DROP THE FRUIT"

Revelation: Our heavenly Father's heart's desire is that we dwell with Him forever and lead others to do the same. His good and healthy fruit in us will cause them to want to eat from the Vine (John 15:1–5) and drink from the Well that never runs dry. Don't drop the fruit!

FEELS SO GOOD TO LAY DOWN

WRITE DOWN WHAT THE HOLY SPIRIT SAYS TO YOU:

LESSON 35

Brother's Keeper

Genesis 4; Proverbs 14:16; Proverbs 14:30; Proverbs 14:29; Proverbs 15:18; Proverbs 18:24; Proverbs 19:18–20; Proverbs 22:24; Proverbs 29:22–23; Matthew 23:11; Luke 22:27; Romans 12:10–21; Romans 16:17; 1 Corinthians 13:4–6; Hebrews 12:7–8; Philippians 2:3–7; 1 John 3:16–18

A dear friend will love you no matter what, and a family sticks together through all kinds of trouble.
—**Proverbs 17:17** TPT

Anyone who loves their brother and sister lives in the light, and there is nothing in them t o make them stumble.
—**1 John 2:10** NIV

There is no doubt that our youngest son, Colton, was born at just the *right time* and was just the *right fit* for our family. Praise the Lord! Before we left Enid, Oklahoma, in 2008, we were fellowshipping with another Air Force couple and their family in their home. I'll never forget, she made the best homemade chicken tacos. As we sat around their dinner table, the faith-filled couple asked if we were planning to grow our family with more children. Shad and I explained that it was definitely our heart's desire to have another child, but we had been waiting on the Lord's perfect timing. There had been a few who had discouraged us from having more children for fear of another child having the same "genetic disorder," but any concern of that in us was overshadowed by the prophetic confirmation of this brother and sister in Christ. Before we left their home, they prayed over Clemmie, laying hands on him and blessing him in Jesus' name. Then they declared something very powerful. They told us we would have another child who would "complete" our family.

We made the move to Maryland in May 2008, and five months later, we found out we were pregnant! When we told this couple the news, they were excited but not surprised. It was just what they had believed and expected along with Clemmie's complete healing. In August 2009 Colton was born. We were grateful for this little baby boy, and Clemmie seemed to be happy about him, too. I was a little concerned, however, about how I would take care of this infant *and* take care of Clem's needs while Shad was away on missions. Clemmie was still having seizures, every day, multiple times a day. We were constantly watching him to make sure he wouldn't fall while having a seizure. Family understood the need to have extra hands, and they came to the rescue. It was a challenging time, but we fully believed our God would take care of all our needs. He did.

One of the first needs He met was providing help in teaching Colt to "self-soothe" and go to sleep on his own. Clemmie was still wanting to be rocked to sleep every night, and I was unsure about how I was going to nurse Colt and get him to sleep while needing to help Clem with his bedtime routine. After spending some time with my mom, dad, and my sister Tonya, who was battling breast cancer at the time, my sister Tara and her youngest flew up to Maryland to help. Tara is very knowledgeable in early childhood development. She has worked with babies in early childhood music classes and is very comfortable with them. She saw my need the first night she was there, took Colt after I nursed him, and laid him down for the night. When she first laid him in the crib, he cried. Tara picked him up, patted his little backside, wrapped him up tightly like a burrito in his blanket, and laid him back down, all while giving a "sh-sh-sh-sh . . ." to soothe him. She repeated it a few more times, teaching him that he would be fine to go to sleep on his own. Eventually, she stopped picking him up from the crib and, instead, would "sh-sh-sh" him, resting her hand softly on him. After just a few repetitions of this, Colt was asleep. And after that *one* night, I never had trouble laying him down to sleep again. It was as if he understood he needed to help Mommy. I will always be grateful for his aunt Tara's help and Colton's independent nature.

Most translations of Proverbs 17:17 end with the words "a brother is *born* for *adversity*." The Hebrew word used here for *adversity* also means "affliction, anguish, distress, tribulation, and trouble." No, this verse does *not* mean that a brother is born to cause trouble, as some might think. Proverbs 17:17 is scriptural evidence that our God *births* or *brings forth* a brother, whether blood kin or a brother in Christ, to help in time of affliction, anguish, distress, tribulation, and trouble. Colt and Clemmie have been that for each other for the past fourteen years now. When Clemmie needs a good laugh, he looks for Colt. When Colt needs a little more gratitude or perspective, he sees what Clemmie endures.

A few years ago, on a Tuesday evening around 7 p.m., Colt witnessed his big brother having a grand-mal seizure. He saw Mommy and Daddy jump into action as his brother struggled to breathe because his jaw was locked up tight, causing his lips to turn blue. He heard us loudly verbalizing instructions to each other from the bathroom to the kitchen and praying aloud as we worked together to keep his big brother safe and bring peace back to his body. "By Jesus' stripes [Clem] you are healed!" (Isaiah 53:5).

Thinking of how traumatic this must be for his twelve-year-old son, Shad told Colt to run across the field to MawMaw's house, where he would find refuge from all the details of what was happening. All he knew now was that his brother was in *distress*. I know he must've prayed a lot. From a distance, he saw the ambulance take his brother away with Mommy following close behind in her own vehicle. Daddy stayed behind to explain to Colt that Clem was now breathing and resting, but he needed to go to the emergency room.

The next Thursday morning, before Colt left for school, without any encouragement, he left a note on the kitchen island for his big brother, who would be returning home from the hospital. After more than forty-eight hours of not seeing his brother, they were reunited again. The doctor's diagnosis was that Clemmie's body had seized due to dangerously low sodium. Clem had been ingesting too much water and gotten sick to his stomach. He had thrown up, causing the sodium level in his body to plummet. This was when his body seized. This seizure was different, though. We had never seen him so violently convulse before this particular Tuesday night, and I pray fervently we never see it again.

I'm thankful for Colt's heart of gratitude instead of self-pity. It would be very easy for him to feel like he's been wronged in some way. In fact, the world highly encourages him to play the victim. When we think of ourselves as mistreated and discriminated against, we begin to think of everyone else as the enemy. We live in the spirit of offense, and that can lead to chaos and calamity in our own lives. Let's look at Cain and Abel's relationship in Genesis 4. We see the two sons of Adam and Eve, two brothers: one a farmer and the other a shepherd. Cain became very angry with Abel and jealous of his favor with the Lord. Abel's only offense was that he had given his best offering to the Lord, and Cain had only given *some* of his crops to the Lord. God was well-pleased with Abel and not so well-pleased with Cain. Here we see the battle between the unrighteousness in Cain and the righteousness in Abel.

The Lord warned Cain about allowing his anger to "rule," or *have power*, over him. It seems he was hot-tempered and unwilling to receive correction—a combination that leads to disaster. The Scripture says, "An angry man stirs up dissention, and a hotheaded one commits many transgressions" (Proverbs 29:22 TLV). There are also many Scriptures that instruct us in being able to receive correction: Proverbs 13:18 says, "Whoever disregards discipline comes to poverty and shame, but whoever heeds correction is honored." Cain disregarded God's correction and killed Abel. When questioned by the Lord concerning the whereabouts of his brother, Cain replied, "I don't know. Am I my brother's keeper?" (Genesis 4:9 TLV). The Hebrew word used for *keeper* here means "to guard, protect, attend to, preserve, regard, and save." The Lord gave a clear answer to how He feels about being our "brother's keeper." His response to the murder of Abel and Cain's arrogant attitude was to banish and curse Cain from the land on which he had killed his brother. The punishment was severe. We still see its implications today.

When God gives us a brother or a sister, He fully expects that we are to be good stewards of what He has given. In other words, *yes*, we *are* to be our brother's keeper. Evidence of an obedient and godly life is to encourage, edify, love, and even correct each other at times. We are to put our brothers' and sisters' needs above our own. Philippians 2:3–4 (TLV) says, "Do nothing out of selfishness or conceit, but with humility consider others as more important than yourselves, looking out not only for your own interests but also for the interests of others." This Christlike, humble posture is completely in opposition to the unsaved world's way of behaving. Kingdom belief is this: "but many who are first will be last, and the last first" (Mark 10:31 NIV). Even Jesus, "though he was God, he did not think of equality with God as something to cling to. Instead, he gave up his divine privileges; he took the humble position of a slave and was born as a human being" (Philippians 2:6–7 NLT). Shouldn't we take a similar humble position?

If we're looking for a reason to feel hurt or victimized, we will find it. The enemy is always willing to remind us of how unfairly we have been treated and how we deserve better. We must choose, however, to be grateful for the things we do have and the opportunities to make the most out of what we've been given to bless our brothers and sisters. "Be thankful in all circumstances, for this is God's will for you who belong to Christ Jesus" (1 Thessalonians 5:18 NLT). Consider this: Have you ever wondered why families with many children are successful in humility and not jealousy? They are actively serving one another. If you want to get your mind off your own problems, go work at a homeless shelter or soup kitchen. Suddenly you might become grateful for what you have and not consumed by what you lack. When we serve others, our own selfish desires become secondary, and hopefully disappear, as we become more like the Father.

First John 3:10–12 (TLV) says, "It is clear who are the children of God and who are the children of the devil by this—anyone who does not act righteously or love his brother is not of God. For this is the message you have heard from the beginning—we should love one another. Do not be like Cain, who was from the evil one and murdered his brother. And why did he murder him? Because his deeds were evil, while his brother's were righteous." We might not go as far as Cain did with Abel and commit murder, but if we have strife and jealousy toward our brother, we are committing murder in our hearts. It is sin that needs repentance.

I believe Colt will continue to know and give compassion simply because he has had little glimpses of the battles Clem has had. He is grateful for life and has already seen how fragile it can be. Do we see things with a thankful heart or with a heart of bitterness and self-pity? I am amazed at those who've truly known various trials and hardships. They are the ones with grateful hearts and compassion for others. We are thankful for Colt's thankful heart and compassion. May he walk in the Spirit, never feeling like a victim, but instead knowing that he and Clem have been given each other in order to proclaim victory in Jesus. Amen!

Revelation: Have the mind of Christ, to keep your brother or sister, not for your benefit but for theirs. Build them up to be all God created them to be, and you will be blessed by God.

FEELS SO GOOD TO LAY DOWN

WRITE DOWN WHAT THE HOLY SPIRIT SAYS TO YOU:

LESSON 36

Overlooking the Heart of God

Exodus 15:20–21; 2 Kings 22:14–20; 2 Chronicles 34:22; Isaiah 8:3; Proverbs 31:26; Luke 8:1–3; Luke 10:38–41; John 4:39–42; John 19:25; Acts 21:9; Romans 8; Romans 16; 1 Corinthians 16:19; Titus 2

> *"And it shall come to pass afterward, that I will pour out my Spirit on all flesh; your sons and your daughters shall prophesy, your old men shall dream dreams, and your young men shall see visions. Even on the male and female servants in those days I will pour out my Spirit."*
> **—Joel 2:28–29** ESV

> *" 'In the last days, God says, I will pour out my Spirit on all people. Your sons and daughters will prophesy, your young men will see visions, your old men will dream dreams. Even on my servants, both men and women, I will pour out my Spirit in those*

days, and they will prophesy.'"
—**Acts 2:17–18** NIV

I would be remiss if I didn't put pen to paper regarding the many things in my adult life that led me to write this book. You have already read many stories concerning being a military wife, a special needs mother, and a boy mom, but there is another ingredient in my calling that has intensified the longing to "lay down." Over forty years of my life have been committed to leading others into the presence of Jesus through music. I truly believe the Lord *knit* a song of praise in my heart with the purpose of bringing others to Him through that song. I have loved every part of learning music and studying it to enable me to give my very best to the Lord. The Lord also placed in my heart a strong passion for *the* Church. I was born into church ministry, and I have experienced the good, bad, and ugly involved in pastoring a church. Regardless, music ministry and evangelism through music is something about which I'm very passionate, but this part of my calling has caused me to become weary at times and in need of rest. This discouragement has not come from preparing the music to bring before the Lord, but rather it comes from a buffeting within the Church. Whether it comes from a misunderstanding of Scripture or reluctance to question tradition and denominational doctrine, it has become more evident that the heart of God is increasingly overlooked. It is my hope to shed *Light* (John 9:5) on the heart of our heavenly Father toward women, and more specifically women in ministry.

Over twenty years ago, when I learned how to *study* Scripture and not just read it, I was taught to examine who penned it, to whom it was written, why it was written, and when it was written. It takes some time to research the history, culture, and context surrounding a passage of Scripture. Although I have never taken a seminary class, I do have the *greatest* Teacher—the Holy Spirit. Second Timothy 2:15 says, "Be diligent to present yourself approved to God, a worker who does not need to be ashamed, rightly dividing the word of truth." The Greek word used for "be diligent" also means "to study, make effort, and labor." This verse could also read as this: "*Study, make a diligent effort,* and *labor* to *prove* yourself to be *acceptable* and *pleasing* to God, *a doer, laborer,* and *worker* who will *not be disgraced, dishonored,* or *ashamed, correctly dissecting* and *cutting* the *words in speech, preaching,* and *teaching* the truth.*"* This is my heart, dear friends. I never want to dishonor my God with what I say, so I must make sure I study His truth diligently in order to never paint an incorrect picture of our God's heart toward *all* His people.

I am greatly concerned that we overlook the heart of God by picking and choosing certain Scriptures that might support our traditions, cultures, or even ungodly lifestyles. Satan himself uses certain Scriptures to tempt us and or give us an incorrect understanding of almighty God. The enemy accuses and divides the body of Christ, misusing the "two-edged sword" (Hebrews 4:12) as a weapon to destroy the work of the Holy Spirit. The devil uses these divisions with the purpose of causing the house to fall and fail. "And if a house is divided against itself, that house will not be able to stand" (Mark 3:25 TLV). So, how do we make certain he does not succeed creating discord among the people of God? God's beloved people *must* grow in the knowledge of Jesus and truly understand the heart of our heavenly Father through His words *and* His actions throughout Scripture.

I am so grateful to live in the time when I now live. It is not an accident that each of us is on this earth right at this very moment. Our Lord *purposed* to have each one of us here, right now. I am thankful to have the Word of God translated into English so that I can study it in my own language. I'm also grateful to have the *Strong's Concordance*, the *Interlinear Bible*, and other resources to help in my study of Scripture. This opportunity was not always available, nor even permissible for women. When Jesus walked the earth, Jewish boys went to school to study and memorize the Torah—the Old Testament Scriptures. Girls were not given that opportunity. I'm grateful to now have access to the living and powerful written Word of God, a privilege many women in Scripture were denied . . . until Jesus. Because women in the Jewish culture were not permitted to learn the Scriptures as the men were permitted, some women turned to idol worship and false gods. When early New Testament churches were birthed, there were still some women who were confused and uneducated in the holy Scriptures. As the Scriptures were being preached, these women would disrupt the gatherings with questions. They were interrupting the services by loudly asking their husbands to interpret the Word of God for them to understand. The apostle Paul speaks to this *lack of order* in the Church, specifically in the church at Corinth (1 Corinthians 14:34–35). Timothy was battling the same *lack of order* and disruptions in his church services in Ephesus (1 Timothy 2:11–12). He was also battling a lack of modesty among some of the women who were new converts. This is an issue that can still be addressed in many of the American churches today.

Not all the New Testament churches battled these issues, and not all issues were caused by disorderly women. Unlike the women in the churches of Corinth and Ephesus, I am so thankful to have a long heritage of godly *studiers* of the Word in my family—both male and female. I'm thankful to have learned early in my life how to read, memorize, and study the Scriptures. I'm thankful for the Holy Spirit, who teaches me these truths. Women all over the world have similar testimonies. We are no longer confused and uneducated in the Word of God. Thank You, Holy Spirit! In fact, some of the best Bible teachers I know are women. I have been involved in numerous Bible studies with women who *crave* the Word of God, walk in the Spirit, and live lives of fasting and prayer. I have personally witnessed faith in these women that would, indeed, *move mountains* (Matthew 17:20).

I love how the Old and New Testaments reveal our God's

heart toward women. Adam was not complete without Eve (Genesis 2:18). They were equal helpmates. That was God's perfect design. Exodus 15 tells of a *prophetess* named Miriam who *led* the women of Israel in *praise and worship* after God delivered them from Egypt and the Red Sea. Deborah, another *prophetess*, was chosen by God as a *judge* and a *military strategist* for the nation of Israel (Judges 4 and 5). Esther was a queen and a *leader* for her people who called all of Israel to fast and pray (Esther 4:16). She found favor with, and had direct access to, the king in order to save the Jewish people, both men and women (Esther 2:9, 17). If Esther would've remained *silent*, her people would have perished. Esther 4:14 (TLV) says, "For if you remain silent at this time, relief and deliverance will arise for the Jews from another place—but you and your father's house will perish. Who knows whether you have attained royal status for such a time as this?" Our God had appointed Esther at just the right time to help save His people from the enemy. If we remain silent, will there be many who will perish and spend eternity without Jesus? These examples are just *some* of the women the Lord equipped and purposed to bring about His will for His people in the Old Testament.

In the New Testament, Anna spent all her elder days preaching at the Temple, where Jesus was circumcised: "Now there was one, Anna, a prophetess, the daughter of Phanuel, of the tribe of Asher. She was of a great age, and had lived with a husband seven years from her virginity; and this woman was a widow of about eighty-four years, who did not depart from the temple, but served God with fastings and prayers night and day. And coming in that instant she gave thanks to the Lord, and spoke of Him to all those who looked for redemption in Jerusalem" (Luke 2:36–38). She proclaimed salvation to those who needed it. Throughout Jesus' three-year earthly ministry, female disciples followed Him and provided for His ministry (Luke 8:1–3). Women were also part of the original seventy sent out two by two to do as Jesus had asked. He instructed the seventy to pray for more workers to evangelize the lost. He also commissioned them to "heal the sick in that town, and say to them, 'The kingdom of God has come near to you'" (Luke 10:2–9 TLV). Jesus told the seventy that if the town did not receive them, they should then go into the streets and declare, "Even the dust of your town sticking to our feet, we wipe off as a witness to you. But know this! The kingdom of God has come near" (Luke 10:11 TLV). Sounds like street preaching to me—and women were included.

I've always been intrigued with the story of Mary and Martha in Luke 10:38–42. Martha was busy serving Jesus and His disciples, but her sister, Mary, was "seated at the Master's feet, listening to His teaching" (Luke 10:39 TLV). Martha became irritated that Mary was not in the kitchen helping her serve. According to tradition, and to Martha's way of thinking, Mary was expected to be on the hospitality team, helping in the kitchen—where women belonged. Martha asked Jesus to rebuke Mary and insist that she help her serve. Jesus did something opposite to culture, tradition, and expectation, however. He expresses to Martha that she should not be bothered by Mary sitting at His feet. You see, Mary was taking the position of a *disciple*. She was learning from the Master. She was abiding in His presence. Mary was worshiping. Culture said this was a position only allowed for men, but Mary, in all sincerity to be taught by her Savior, challenged tradition and culture. Was Martha upset because she needed help serving the Lord, or was she perturbed with Mary because she was doing something countercultural and contrary to tradition? Jesus' response beautifully reveals the heart of our Father: "Mary has chosen what is better, and it will not be taken away from her" (Luke 10:41–42 NIV). Thank You, Jesus! Ladies, taking the position of a disciple, sitting at the Master's feet, is worship that will never be discouraged or rebuked by our Lord.

Jesus continued to reveal the heart of God by doing things contrary to culture and tradition. When we look at John 4, where Jesus met with the woman at the well, we see one of His longest one-on-one conversations recorded in Scripture. When His disciples returned to see Him talking to this woman, Scripture says, "They were amazed that He was speaking with a woman" (John 4:27 TLV). They *marveled*, *wondered*, and *admired* Jesus for speaking with this woman. The disciples were learning the heart of God. John 4:39 tells us that many Samaritans believed in Jesus because of this woman's testimony. She couldn't resist telling others about her Savior. She preached, and she evangelized. History says that this woman was martyred for leading others to Jesus. She would not be silent about what her Savior had done for her. I understand this fully, and I hope you do too.

"'And it shall come to pass in the last days, says God, that I will pour out of My Spirit on all flesh; your sons and your daughters shall prophesy, your young men shall see visions, your old men shall dream dreams. And on My menservants and on My maidservants I will pour out My Spirit in those days; and they shall prophesy" (Acts 2:17–18). In the Upper Room, where over 120 men, women, and children met, the Holy Spirit *gushed out* and was *exceedingly bestowed* on every last one of them. Peter recognized this fulfillment of Joel 2:28 and knew it was time to go to work. Are we not in the last days even now? Most assuredly, we are in the *latter* of the last days. How can any of God's people stay quiet when the souls of many are in danger of an eternity without Jesus? It's time to stop limiting the Holy Spirit by using only half the Church to preach the Gospel to every creature. Is the Great Commission not for *all*? "And He said to them, 'Go into all the world and preach the gospel to every creature'" (Mark 16:15).

Paul himself spoke approvingly of the women he labored alongside for the cause of Christ. The Holy Spirit spoke through him as he penned Romans 16 and immediately began to "commend" Phoebe. Romans 16:1 (NKJV) says, "I commend to you Pheobe our sister, who is a servant of the church in Cenchrea." If we study the words and the Greek transliterations, *commend* means that Paul is "standing with, by, and up" for Phoebe, "approving her" and "introducing her favorably." This word denotes a "close association, companionship, and union." It also suggests that Paul is "approving" her for an "appointment, establishment, or covenant." *Strong's* defines *servant* as "an attendant, a Christian teacher, pastor, deacon, minister, and servant." Why would Paul need to commend and stand up for Phoebe? Verse 2 says, "that you may receive her in the Lord in a manner worthy of the saints, and assist her in whatever business she has need of you." Could this have been a problem in the church for Paul to have to encourage the church to receive this female minister and help her with whatever she needed? Paul was reminding the church to *receive* Phoebe as Jesus would receive her—seeing beyond the physical and straight to her heart, godly character, and faithful ministry. This might have been contrary to tradition and culture, but Paul instructed them as inspired by the Holy Spirit. That is the heart of God and a "manner worthy of the saints." They were to not only *receive* her, but they were to *assist, aid, stand beside*, and *be readily at hand* to *help* and *provide* for whatever she needed. Could some of these folks have intended to stand in the way of and hinder Phoebe's ministry? That is quite possible, but that is *not* a "manner worthy of the saints."

Paul continued in Romans 16 to advocate for his *co-laborers*: "Greet Priscilla and Aquila, my fellow workers in Christ Jesus, who risked their own necks for my life, to whom not only I give thanks, but also all the churches of the Gentiles. Likewise greet the church that is in their house" (Romans 16:3–5). This wife-and-husband team were sharing the Gospel alongside Paul, even in the face of death. They were also *pastoring* a church in their own home. In Paul's Holy Spirit–inspired writings, there was no differentiation in title or status for this couple. It is interesting, though, that he mentioned Priscilla *first* in his writings. More importantly, though, Paul was thankful for the fearless conviction found in both Priscilla and Aquila. Fearless conviction to live for Jesus and magnify His name should be the standard by which all of us should be considered in the body of Christ.

Paul continued to instruct the church to "*greet*" other fellow workers. The Greek word used for *greet* means "to enfold in the arms, to salute, to welcome, and embrace." Evidently, Paul wanted the church to make this a top priority. Mary was another female who "*labored, toiled, and became weary and fatigued*" for the sake of the Gospel. Junia was also a Roman Christian who was imprisoned with Paul, along with her husband, Andronicus. Paul mentioned that both Andronicus and Junia were "notable among the apostles" (Romans 16:7). Tryphena, Tryphosa, and Persis were to be greeted as they also "labored in the Lord." Paul listed Rufus's mother, Julia, Nereus's sister, and "all the saints who are with them" (Romans 16:15). Needless to say, Paul had a deep respect for all his fellow laborers, many of which were women.

Oh, how we need men like Paul in the Church today to *commend* fellow workers in the Lord, especially women who have a heart *completely devoted* to the calling of the Lord Jesus! It is He who has made them *apostles*, *prophets*, *evangelists*, *pastors*, and *teachers* (Ephesians 4:11). He *never* says these gifts are not for women. We see *all* these positions being filled by women in the Word of God. So, why are we divided on these issues? Has our God changed? No. He is perfect, and He does not change (Malachi 3:6). We are the ones needing to be changed from the inside out. Our hearts must align with God's heart. We must develop eyes to see how He sees. This will take a change of mind—repentance. "Do not be conformed to this world, but be transformed by the renewal of your mind, that by testing you may discern what is the will of God, what is good and acceptable and perfect" (Romans 12:2 ESV).

Having seen and heard the issues hurting the Church today, I wholeheartedly believe we need women *pastoring* women. The issues women have cannot be adequately addressed by men who cannot empathize with them, and, believe me, there are many of these issues. The second chapter of the book of Titus speaks to this matter. Mature women in Christ must mentor less mature women. This is not only scriptural, but completely sensible. I have seen the results of male pastors trying to counsel women who have been abused by their fathers, left by their husbands, or mistreated sexually by men. When a male pastor tries to heal a female's wounds, he then becomes her savior. I have witnessed this firsthand. If these same male pastors would have been able to lead these troubled women to a female pastor, many of the problems of sexual misconduct among pastors would be avoided. Females know best how to speak to females, and males know best how to speak to males. Unfortunately, that is human nature and how flesh responds to flesh, especially to those who do not remain vigilant against the weapons of the enemy.

On the other hand, I believe when we get to heaven, there will be no distinction between the two genders. We will see as God sees and walk in truth. It is written in Galatians 3:28 (TPT) that "we no longer see each other in our former state—Jew or non-Jew, rich or poor, male or female—because we're all one through our union with Jesus Christ." Paul states that, by faith in Jesus Christ, we are no longer separated and divided by how culture and tradition dictates. We are one body working in unity. If the Church truly believed this Scripture, the Gospel of Jesus Christ would go farther faster, and more of the lost would be saved. Why must we wait until heaven when the heart of the Father is so obviously clear throughout His Word? Let's start here and now.

If we were to truly live as Jesus lived and see the redeemed as God sees them, the "gates of hell shall not prevail" (Matthew 16:18 ESV) against the people of God. The Church in one accord would be blessed, and the world would take notice. "But the LORD said to Samuel, 'Do not look at his appearance or at his physical stature, because I have refused him. For the LORD does not see as man sees; for man looks at the outward appearance, but the Lord looks at the heart'" (1 Samuel 16:7). How much more effective would we be if we stopped looking at the exterior and instead looked at the interior—the heart, actions, and character of a follower of Jesus Christ? John 7:24 (TLV) says, "Do not judge by appearance, but judge righteously." We are to *decide* and *distinguish rightly* according to how our God judges, not by the outward appearance and standards of men. I pray we comprehend the heart of God just as Peter did in Acts 10:34–35 (TLV): "I truly understand that God is not one to show favoritism, but in every nation the one who fears Him and does what is right is acceptable to Him." Women of God, continue in reverent fear of the Lord and do what is right in *His* sight. I encourage you to follow the calling of our Lord Jesus Christ. Listen to His voice. Understand how important you are in spreading the Gospel. Your calling, and the spiritual gifts you've been given, are needed to help the Bride get ready for her Bridegroom. The harvest truly is plentiful, but the laborers are few. Do not grow weary in laboring for your Master. You always have a place at His table, in Jesus' name.

Revelation: When we are clothed in the righteousness of Christ Jesus, there is no distinction between male and female. Our God only sees the character of Jesus in us. What is important to God is obedience to His Commission to take the Good News to the ends of the earth, no matter the vessel used to take it.

WRITE DOWN WHAT THE HOLY SPIRIT SAYS TO YOU:

LESSON 37

The Joy of Disentanglement

Psalm 16:11; Psalm 126:5; Isaiah 55:12;
John 15:11; Romans 12:12; Galatians 5:1;
Philippians 4:4; 2 Peter 2:20

Let my passion for life be restored, tasting joy in every breakthrough you bring to me. Hold me close to you with a willing spirit that obeys whatever you say.
—**Psalm 51:12** TPT

Romans 15:13 NIV, "May the God of hope fill you with all joy and peace as you trust in Him, so that you may overflow with hope by the power of the Holy Spirit."
—**Romans 15:13** NIV

Anyone who has ever spent more than twenty-four hours as a patient in a hospital room might understand how restrictive it can be. Being hooked up to a monitor will certainly limit where you can go, how far you can go, and how much you can move. Now imagine being under ten years old and having to be restricted to a small space with all those cords attached to you for over forty-eight hours. Imagine over twenty EEG electrodes glued to your head to monitor your brain activity. Our son Clemmie has had this procedure done several times, and every time a neurologist has ordered one, anxiety would begin to rise up in each of us. Nevertheless, when battles of anxiety and worry begin, we must declare God's Word to win. Philippians 4:6 (TLV) says, "Do not be anxious about anything—but in everything, by prayer and petition with thanksgiving, let your requests be made known to God." So, we would take our concerns to the Lord, trusting that *Jehovah-nissî*—meaning "the Lord Our Banner" (Exodus 17:15)—had already gone before us to provide for us and bring peace into that hospital room. Our worry would turn into praise and gratitude for all Jesus had *already done* and would continue to do.

Evidence of our God's provision was there in how the hospital staff was always so gracious, kind, and gentle with Clem. The names and faces of many of the nurses and technicians will stay in our memories for a long time. Many of those nurses and techs would acknowledge Clemmie's easygoing demeanor throughout his hospital stay, which was even more evidence of the Lord's peace and provision. We have endeavored never to miss an opportunity to testify of the reason we are calm in the midst of chaos and joyful in the midst of distress. We give all glory to Jesus.

Shad and I would sing to Clem at times when he would get a little upset. That is what you do for your child when he is afraid, and that is what our heavenly Father does for His children. He sings songs of joy over us to quiet our souls. Zephaniah 3:17 (NLT) says, "For the LORD your God is living among you. He is a mighty savior. He will take delight in you with gladness. With his love, he will calm all your fears. He will rejoice over you with joyful songs." How wonderful to be able to illustrate this Scripture for our son and to the hospital staff. Clemmie's favorite song is "My Jesus, I Love Thee." He has wanted that song to be played in his bedroom every night since he was seven and a half months old, and so that is the song we would sing many times in those hospital rooms. Talk about testifying! We also understood that our praise would shut the mouth of the enemy (Psalm 8:2), and our adversary needed to be silenced.

I've heard it said that it is in our darkest moments when God's glory shines brightest. If we believe this, then hospital rooms are the ideal place to bring to light God's power working in us. At the same time that the forty-eight-hour EEG was recording Clemmie's brain activity through the electrodes on his head, we were also being recorded on video. Every move Clem made was being recorded to see how his body responded during a seizure. So, we were having to keep him in front of the camera at all times. If he went too far out of view for more than a couple of minutes, we would be reminded by the nursing staff, or the video camera moving to find him, to bring him back into view. Everything we did in this forty-eight-hours was on display for the doctors and nurses to see. They watched as Clem ate, as he played, and as he slept, and, of course, that meant that *we* were being observed, as well. How we responded to a seizure, stress, discomfort, or fatigue would reveal the depth of our confidence in the Redeemer whom we claimed to love in our song. "Don't be dejected and sad, for the joy of the LORD is your strength!" (Nehemiah 8:10 NLT). The Hebrew word for *joy* in this verse means "rejoicing" and "gladness." How can we show others rejoicing and gladness? One way to display the joy of the Lord is to sing joyful songs.

Another way to demonstrate joy and gladness is to laugh. We've all heard it said that "laughter is the best medicine." Did you know that is not only a scientific fact, but a biblical truth? Proverbs 17:22 (TLV) says, "A cheerful heart is good medicine, but a crushed spirit dries up the bones." Being in a hospital room does not *naturally* bring about much jubilation and laughter, especially for a child, but we serve a *supernatural* God, who gives an *abundance* of joy in His presence (Psalm 16:11). This divine abundance was apparent after Clemmie would walk around in circles during his forty-eight-hour EEG. He would only be able to walk so far with all the leads attached, but at least they gave him plenty of rope to roam a little. We would watch Mr. Clem walk and turn right, then walk and turn right. This happened over and over again. The right turns eventually led to a tangled cord that needed to be untangled to free Clem up to roam again. So, my husband would pick Clem up in his strong arms, then turn to the left over and over again in order to unravel the cord. This became something Clemmie really looked forward to doing with Daddy. As soon as Shad would pick him up, Clem would burst into laughter. His laughter was so contagious that we would laugh along with him. The hospital staff would laugh. That hospital hallway would be filled with our precious child's laughter for all to hear. I can only imagine Clemmie's displeasure if he had stayed tangled up, restrained to never leave his bed where the machine monitoring him was positioned. There would've been no laughter, only tears.

Our Abba Father has done the same for those who have received His precious Son, Jesus, as Savior and Lord. Sin had us entangled us, confining us to our death bed. Daddy came to us, picked us up in His strong arms, and freed us. Now, having experienced this gracious act of love, we are no longer to spin in circles returning to the snare that kept us imprisoned. Instead, we are to keep our eyes fixed on Jesus, who makes our paths straight, and we are to confidently declare that "at last we have freedom, for Christ has set us free! We must always cherish this truth and firmly refuse to go back into the bondage of our past" (Galatians 5:1 TPT).

How do we "firmly refuse to go back into the bondage of our past"? We must wholeheartedly believe we have complete liberty in Jesus by the power of His Spirit and armed with His truth. This is so important in order for us to no longer be enslaved by sin (Romans 6:6). Likewise, knowing what Jesus suffered to purchase our complete freedom should generate in us an unending desire to remain free of what originally took us captive. When we are fully aware of the price paid for our freedom, and that there is an Enemy waging war against us (1 Peter 5:8), we put on the whole armor of God and become warriors to protect that freedom. Any experience on the battlefield will produce a warrior or soldier who stands guard watching attentively for an attack on that blood-bought freedom. Staying alert is serious business to the experienced soldier—a matter of life or death. A seasoned soldier also knows to follow his commander's orders at the moment the command is given and according to every detail of that command. This is critical on the battlefield. Second Timothy 2:4 (TLV) says, "No one serving as a soldier entangles himself in the activities of everyday life, so that he might please the one who enlisted him." A true soldier of the Lord will remain vigilant to evade the traps of the Enemy. When we avoid being ensnared, we are free to move, or more importantly, the Holy Spirit is free to move in us. When He is free to move in us, He can produce His beautiful fruit in abundance. Rejoice and be glad!

Those hospital rooms would've been void of laughter had it not been for the strong, safe arms of a loving father ready to untangle his child from something that would cause him misery and loss of joy. Aren't we grateful for that kind of unfailing love? Aren't we thankful for a heavenly Father who is an "ever-present help" for His children (Psalm 46:2 TLV)? The joy of Jesus was in those hospital rooms as we remained confident of our heavenly Father's promises. His presence has been unmistakable in each of those forty-eight-hour stays, not only for us, but hopefully, also for the doctors, nurses, and staff.

How many more people would we touch for Jesus Christ if we would only rejoice in the midst of trouble? "The LORD is my rock, my fortress, and my savior; my God is my rock, in whom I find protection. He is my shield, the power that saves me, and my place of safety" (Psalm 18:2 NLT). Who wouldn't find joy in that truth? He is faithful to bring comfort and joy in the most difficult times. My prayer is that we would continue to act as we believe, confident in our Savior and boasting in His strength as we are filled with His joy.

Revelation: Satan wants us to go around and around in our sin and become entangled. Our heavenly Father wants to untangle us as we abide safely in His arms and cast all our cares upon Him. It is there we find freedom and joy!

FEELS SO GOOD TO LAY DOWN

WRITE DOWN WHAT THE HOLY SPIRIT SAYS TO YOU:

LESSON 38

Growth Spurts

Ecclesiastes 1:18; 1 Corinthians 14:20; Ephesians 4:14–15; Philippians 3:15; Hebrew 5:13; Hebrews 6:1; 1 Peter 2:2; 2 Peter 3:18

> *"But to you who fear My name the Sun of Righteousness shall arise with healing in His wings; and you shall go out and grow fat like stall-fed calves."*
> **—Malachi 4:2**

> *But solid food is for the mature, who through practice have their senses trained to discern both good and evil.*
> **—Hebrews 5:14** TLV

It was Sunday morning, February 6, 1983. I woke up that morning excited to ask Mom and Dad questions about Jesus becoming *my* personal Savior and Lord. As the grandchild of two preachers and the child of pastors/evangelizers, Jesus had been the overall focus in our lives.

I had witnessed full dedication to serving the Lord, and I'd seen my parents and grandparents lead others to salvation through Jesus. On this Sunday morning, however, *I* heard Him knocking, and I opened the door. I prayed, thanking Him for dying on the cross for my sins, asking Him to forgive me of my sins, and then asking him to "come into my heart." "For God so loved the world that He gave His one and only Son, that whoever believes in Him shall not perish but have eternal life" (John 3:16 TLV). After we said, "Amen," I remember jumping up to touch the beam that hung on our ceiling. I was overjoyed!

That day I came to my Jesus as a child, simply believing that I needed Him to save me from my sins so that I would go to heaven one day. Romans 3:23 (TLV) says, "For all have sinned and fall short of the glory of God," and, at eight years old, I was no different. I knew I needed saving. I trusted that Jesus was exactly who I'd heard about, and I trusted my parents' instruction leading me to Him. This was *simple, childlike faith.* That day I was reconciled back to God, and my name was written in the Lamb's Book of Life (Revelation 20:15). Soon after, I was water-baptized by my dad. "The baptism of repentance," as Scripture calls it in Luke 3:16 and Acts 19:4, was part of my obedience to the Lord and a public display of my confession of faith in Jesus Christ. Praise the Lord! However, this was only the beginning of my relationship with Jesus. Just like the milestones of growth we look for in our children after they are born, we have milestones of growth we should meet after we are reborn in Christ. I had no idea how and when these milestones, or *growth spurts*, would come, but my God, in His perfect plan for me, had all my days written and ordained for me before I was even born.

At *eight years old*, my relationship with the Lord would be more about getting to know Him through Scripture and song, mostly in the different classes and programs at church. I don't remember having a "quiet time" with God in which I just wanted to be alone with Him and abide in His presence. My time with Him was spent with others around. I loved Jesus, but my relationship with Him was corporate, not intimate. As a child, I had no understanding of intimacy. At this point, it was a relationship motivated by fear and respect. In fact, it was most likely a fear of hell that initially compelled me to ask Jesus to be my Savior. I was glad to go to heaven when I died. "The fear of the LORD is the beginning of wisdom, and the knowledge of the Holy One is understanding" (Proverbs 9:10). Just as a child must first *respect, reverence*, and *fear* her earthly parents, understanding their position and authority, a child of the King of kings and Lord of lords must first come to *respect, reverence*, and *fear* the Lord's position and authority over us. This is how becoming wise in His will and ways must start.

As a child I memorized Scripture and told others what I knew about Jesus. There was an initial excitement about my salvation, and I wanted everyone to be saved and go to heaven. Just as I sought to obey and please my earthly parents, I sought to obey and please the One who had given me eternal life. As a devoted rule-follower, I gave attention to the rules and strived never to break them. "Your word have I treasured in my heart that I might not sin against You" (Psalm 119:11). I believed like a child who had not yet experienced trials and troubles in life. It was a pure faith but untested. This was a good start and would prove to be the foundation I needed to build my faith, brick upon brick.

Seven years later, at fifteen years old, trials, tribulations, and troubles did come, and they hit our family very hard. I was confronted with and affected by the consequences of sins that I did not commit. Because I loved my family and wanted to honor them, I felt it was my duty to help take care of their needs. Conversely, I had been taken away from everything I'd known in Florida as we made the move to Dallas, Texas. Some might've considered this a time when I might have been "justified" to rebel against God and all authority, but I was kept from rebellion. The Word I had treasured in my heart was the solid foundation saving me from my making my own ungodly choices. I was now beginning to *apply* the head knowledge I had, and I was experiencing God's faithfulness and deep love. My heart was now engaged in my relationship with God through His Son, and time alone with Him became a priority. In this very difficult time for my family, God became more than Someone I read about and the One to whom I prayed merely at mealtimes and bedtimes. He became my "Abba."

GROWTH SPURTS

Romans 8:15 (TLV) says, "For you did not receive the spirit of slavery to fall again into fear; rather, you received the Spirit of adoption, by whom we cry, 'Abba! Father!'" Like a daddy comforting His child, He was the One to whom I ran when just about all of what I had known was suddenly taken away. During this time, I also learned "it is better to take refuge in Adonai than to trust in man" (Psalm 118:8 TLV). By reevaluating in whom I placed my confidence, I was getting to know Him, not just in word, but in His tender love and care. He was *my* salvation and help in time of need. Ministry through music, and nurturing the talents He'd given, was very important in these years. Music ministry with my sisters was also how the Holy Spirit was healing my wounded soul. He was revealing Himself to me gently so that I would recognize Him better in my next growth spurt.

Seven years later, at twenty-two years old, I was in my last few semesters at the University of North Texas when I received a call from an older college peer. She asked if we could meet for supper, and I agreed to meet her at a local restaurant. As we sat having a meal together, she described a dream she'd had. In the dream, the Lord asked her to pray over me to be filled with the Holy Spirit (Acts 8:15–17; Acts 19:1–6). She was sure this was about making my ministry with my sisters more effective. She only saw in part because He was going to do so much more. I am reminded of Acts 9, when the Lord appeared to Ananias in a vision and asked him to go to Saul, who had a vision of

Ananias "laying his hands on him, so that he might regain his sight" (Acts 9:12 TLV). Ananias did as the Lord Jesus asked of him, and when he got to Saul, whom he called "brother," he told him the Lord had sent him "that you may see again and be filled with the Holy Spirit" (Acts 9:17 NIV). Saul was only expecting Ananias to help him regain his sight, but God wanted to do more. I believe Saul had already repented and turned his life over to Jesus. In fact, the Lord told Ananias that Saul was praying. Ananias was not sent to tell Saul about Jesus. Jesus Himself appeared to Saul revealing exactly who He was. Ananias was not sent to say a prayer of salvation with Saul. I believe Saul had already done that in sincerity to the Lord. Instead, I believe Ananias was sent as a witness to Saul's complete surrender, and he was sent to be a conduit of healing and anointing from the Holy Spirit. This had to be done to fulfill his calling in taking the Good News of Jesus Christ to the Gentiles *and* because Saul would have to suffer much for Jesus. Only the Holy Spirit could bring him through all that he was about to endure for the cause of Christ. "So Ananias went and found Saul. He laid his hands on him and said, 'Brother Saul, the Lord Jesus, who appeared to you on the road, has sent me so that you might regain your sight and be filled with the Holy Spirit.' Instantly something like scales fell from Saul's eyes, and he regained his sight. Then he got up and was baptized" (Acts 9:17–18 NIV).

Like Saul, who would later be known as Paul, I was a rule follower and had many Scriptures memorized. I considered myself knowledgeable of the Bible and in good standing with God. It would've been very easy for me to be like a Pharisee, being led by the Law but not by the Spirit. "But if you are led by the Spirit, you are not under the law" (Galatians 5:18 ESV). I might have spent my time wounding and persecuting those who did not believe as I did, making Scripture into a sword to swing to hurt and not to heal. I am still conscientious to crucify that fleshly desire to prove people wrong and condemn them for their sins, understanding that I must first remove that ungodly plank from my own eye (Matthew 7:3).

Unlike the Pharisees, however, I was saved. I had recognized the Messiah, and I had a saving encounter with Jesus, even though it wasn't a road-to-Damascus experience. However, the Lord knew I would need humility, and I would need His power to reach the lost and hurting. This is when He gave my Spirit-filled college friend the dream. I was not offended by her dream and her invitation to be baptized in the Spirit. I trusted her discernment after I had witnessed her godly life on display at the College of Music. I must've been ready at twenty-two years old to humbly say yes to being filled with the Holy Spirit because I didn't hesitate to submit. I wanted anything and everything He wanted me to have, even if it meant doing something beyond the comfort of tradition and religion.

In a small apartment just off campus, I surrendered to the Holy Spirit as other believers laid hands on me and prayed for me to walk in the anointing. Paul did this with the disciples. Acts 19 refers to it as "the baptism of the Holy Spirit." I was being equipped to "go into all the world" with *His* power and *His* authority, but was I desperate to use His power yet? Not so much. However, this did change the way I worshiped. I began worshiping unhindered, not concerned about what others thought. My worship was about Him, to Him, and for Him alone. My *sight was being restored to see* who *the Holy Spirit* was and how He was moving. I was becoming acquainted with the Helper sent to do "greater works" in and through me (John 14). I now had experiences with God the Father, God the Son, *and* God the Holy Spirit.

Seven years later, at twenty-nine years old, in desperation I learned that God in three Persons truly *is* the "same yesterday, today, and forever" (Hebrews 13:8). "He changes not" (Malachi 3:6). He speaks today just as He did throughout all of Scripture. Abiding in His presence was key to survival and strength. Being still (Psalm 46:10) and listening to Him, instead of talking, was imperative. I became the mother of a child who needed physical healing, and I was going to do anything and everything to see it come to pass "on earth as it is in heaven." At this time, I believe the immersion in the Holy Spirit that I had received seven years prior became activated by humility and desperation. I craved abiding in His presence. I couldn't get enough of digging deep into His Word. I learned how to really study Scripture, and it became alive to me. This is also when I began hearing His voice instantly and sometimes audibly.

I truly loved my Lord, *all* of Him. His heart, from Genesis to Revelation, became very evident to me, and it still does today.

Though twenty-one years have passed since this last major growth spurt, He is not done yet! I continue to "work out my salvation" (Philippians 2:12), knowing that "He who began a good work in me will perfect it until the day of Christ Jesus" (Philippians 1:6). My compassion for others and empathy toward the lost continues to grow moment by moment, but my passion to share the truth grows also. Now, at the age of fifty, I see my Lord through a much wider scope. He is Creator, Judge, Father, and Redeemer. He is Power and Might, and He is Healer and my Help in time of trouble. He is also my Joy and Friend, and I am grateful to be His for eternity. Unlike that Sunday morning on February 6, 1983, He no longer just has my heart. As I grow in understanding *all* of Him, He becomes *Lord over all* of me. May we all know the "fullness of Him who fills all in all" (Ephesians 1:23).

Revelation: Growth spurts are essential in our relationship with the Lord. In order to grow, we must remain fed and nourished. Expect to outgrow things and relationships that once fit. Growth spurts can be painful, but growing in Christ is always worth the temporary discomfort.

FEELS SO GOOD TO LAY DOWN

WRITE DOWN WHAT THE HOLY SPIRIT SAYS TO YOU:

_____

_____

_____

_____

_____

_____

_____

_____

_____

_____

_____

_____

_____

_____

_____

_____

_____

_____

_____

_____

LESSON 39

A "Chord" of Three Strands

Genesis 40:18; Exodus 37:18; Joshua 2:18;
1 Chronicles 13:8; Matthew 12:40

A person standing alone can be attacked and defeated, but two can stand back-to-back and conquer. Three are even better, for a triple-braided cord is not easily broken.
—**Ecclesiastes 4:12** NLT

"For where two or three are gathered together in My name, there I am in their midst."
—**Matthew 18:20** TLV

There is something very special about the number three. The Hebrew word for "three," *shelosh*, means "*new life, harmony,* and *wholeness.*" In Scripture, the number *three* represents what is *complete*. Think of God—the Father, the Son, and the Holy Spirit. How about the Jewish patriarchs:

Abraham, Isaac, and Jacob? Why *three* gifts from the *three* Magi? And why did the Holy Spirit wait until the *third* day to raise Jesus from that grave? The apostle Paul went *three* days without sight, and Jonah spent *three* days in the belly of the whale. We could dive more deeply into these truths, but I'll save that for another time, or maybe even another book. For now, let us understand that *three* is very significant in *completing* His will on earth as it is in heaven. "For there are *three* that bear witness in heaven: the Father, the Word, and the Holy Spirit; and these *three* are one" (1 John 5:7).

I am the oldest of *three* girls. There are certain personality traits that come with being the oldest, and my sisters would agree that I have many of them. Most of the time, the oldest is a take-charge, single-strand kind of person who works alone to get things done. I can definitely testify that the battle is real in striving toward perfection. However, we are all three very close in age. Eleven months after I was born, my middle sister, Tonya, entered the world. Twenty months after Tonya, our youngest sister, Tara, arrived. At one point, our parents had *three* girls all under *three* years old. I get tired just thinking about it! Since I was only an eleven-month-old baby when Tonya arrived (two to three months old when my parents began preparing for her arrival), there was no jealousy or competing for Mom and Dad's attention. With Tara arriving before I was *three* years old, it was "all hands on deck" in the Hayneses' home. From the very beginning, I knew I needed to be a helper for my mom and dad. I remember Dad pulling over on one of our long holiday road trips from Florida to Mississippi in the family station wagon. With the back hatch open, my mom changed the diaper of one sister, and my dad changed the diaper of the other. Observing all this, I stood up and changed my own diaper, even though I was mostly potty-trained. I didn't do this out of anger or bitterness toward my parents, who had their hands full. Rather, it was because I loved my mom and dad. I felt a sense of duty to be their helper. Mom and Dad recently reminded me of a quote from one of our favorite movies. They said, "You were born older, Tiffany." The Lord had woven a sense of responsibility into me from the very beginning. "My frame was not hidden from You when I was made in the secret place, when I was woven together in the depths of the earth" (Psalm 139:15). However, the Lord was preparing me to be more than just a single strand. He gave me two other strengthening strands, and we would need to be tightly woven together in order to be *unbreakable* for our Lord Jesus.

By the time we were all *three* out of diapers, the *three* of us were learning to sing with each other. With the help of Mom and Dad, Tara would sing the melody, Tonya would sing low alto, and I would sing high tenor. To this day, we joke about how wise Mom and Dad were in teaching us to harmonize with each other in order to keep us from fussing and fighting. Their desire for a trio who would sing and play stringed instruments came after they heard the Stone Brothers in concert in the early 1970s. These *three* brothers who sang and played trumpets inspired Mom and Dad to go home and ask the Lord for their own musical trio. My parents had already spent years ministering to churches through music and leading young people into deeper relationships with Jesus Christ. They were delighting in Him, and He gave them the desires of their hearts (Psalm 37:4). By the time we were in our early teen years, we were traveling to different churches to sing and play our stringed instruments for the Lord. It is a ministry we still have today. Is it any wonder that the Hebrew word for *three* can also be defined as "*a musical instrument,*" specifically "*a three-stringed lute*"? If you know anything about music, you know that a "chord" is at least *three* notes combined *harmoniously*. The word *chord* comes from the French word for *agreement*. How wonderful that *three* sisters can work in *agreement* to praise our God in *three*-part *harmony* in voice and stringed instruments!

Though our ministry of *three* started with music, our Lord, through His transformative power, has made it so much more. Each of us made personal decisions at young ages to receive the free gift of salvation through the precious atoning *blood* of Jesus Christ. Each of us followed Him in *water* baptism, signifying the "old" being buried and the "new" being raised up to *new life* in Christ. And each of us has received the *Holy Spirit* to walk in the power of God and do "greater works" in Jesus' name (John 14:12). The *three* of us had to make our own personal decision to follow the One we were proclaiming in song, and that has made all the difference. "And there are three that bear witness on earth: the Spirit, the water, and the blood; and these three agree as one" (1 John 5:8). In order for our ministry (*His* ministry through us) to be effective and *complete*, all *three* of us had to come into *agreement*, bearing witness on earth of the *blood*, the *water*, and the *Spirit*. This is when our heavenly Father began revealing the unbreakable cord. If one did not agree on these three, then "the strand" would be easily broken.

There is nothing more powerful on earth than a *blood*-bought, *water*-baptized, and Holy *Spirit*-filled three-stranded cord, especially a cord that sings and makes music to the Lord. Satan hates everything about this kind of cord. If he can divide the cord into single strands, then he can overtake and defeat each individual strand. "If a kingdom is divided against itself, that kingdom cannot stand. And if a house is divided against itself, that house cannot stand" (Mark 3:24–25). He has done his very best to divide and isolate us. There have been assassination attempts on our lives at birth, through breast cancer and other illnesses. He's tried to steal our joy through miscarriages, health issues with our children, and major spiritual warfare against our kids. And there has been the warfare to try to destroy the sacred covenant of marriage in our lives. All these schemes of the wicked one were meant to unravel the *cord* of strength almighty God had beautifully pieced together. All these evil plans were done to silence the *chord* that will help bring people into a saving knowledge of our

Lord Jesus Christ. The enemy's schemes will fail as long as the *cord*, and *chord*, of *three* strands remains tightly interwoven around a "scarlet thread"—who is Jesus. One of our favorite verses is Matthew 18:20, where Jesus says, "For where two or three are gathered in My name, I am there in the midst of them." We usually declare this verse right before we sing a song called "In This Very Room," by Ron and Carol Harris. This beautiful song speaks of His promise to be *among*, *before*, and *between* His people who gather in Jesus' name. The result of our Lord Jesus being in our midst and "in this very room" is love, joy, hope, and power to "chase away any gloom." Imagine if the people of God were all tightly woven together, in *agreement*, declaring the Gospel of Jesus. "All the powers of hell will not conquer it" (Matthew 16:18). That would be one very thick, unbreakable cord! If Jesus Christ was truly among His people as we gather, "we demolish arguments and every pretension that sets itself up against the knowledge of God, and we take captive every thought to make it obedient to Christ" (2 Corinthians 10:5 NIV). Every petty argument would cease, and the Kingdom of God would expand. This is the Church the Bridegroom desires.

I am beyond grateful that the Lord gave me two other strands so that I would not have to stand alone in this world. My sisters have locked shields of faith with me on numerous occasions. They have agreed with me on earth in prayer (Matthew 18:19), and I have seen the Holy Spirit move as a result of those prayers of agreement. I not only value them as sisters in blood, but I value them as sisters in the Spirit. May we continue until *completion* to be *three* strands tightly woven into one for His honor and glory, and may Jesus be at the center of all God's people.

FEELS SO GOOD TO LAY DOWN

A "CHORD" OF THREE STRANDS

Revelation: Find two or more people with whom you can stand in agreement in Jesus name. That threefold cord, bound together with blood, water, and Spirit, will be very difficult to break!

FEELS SO GOOD TO LAY DOWN

WRITE DOWN WHAT THE HOLY SPIRIT SAYS TO YOU:

LESSON 40

Why the Delay?

Lamentations 3:25–26; Psalm 27:3; Psalm 37:7, 9; Psalm 37:34; Psalm 62:5; Psalm 130:5–6; Proverbs 20:22; Isaiah 8:17; Isaiah 40:31; Habakkuk 2:3; Micah 7:7; Romans 8:25; Philippians 3:20; Hebrew 9:28; James 5:7

Wait on the Lord; be of good courage, and He shall strengthen your heart; wait, I say, on the Lord!
—**Psalm 27:14**

My brethren, count it all joy when you fall into various trials, knowing that the testing of your faith produces patience. But let patience have its perfect work, that you may be perfect and complete, lacking nothing.
—**James 1:2–4**

From the time we were given the diagnosis of a "rare genetic disorder" for our son, we were desperate for wisdom from our heavenly Father. When your child is sick or hurting, you become a resolute warrior, ready to take on whatever is coming against him. It is very easy to feel helpless when the "weapon formed" (Isaiah 54:17) against your child is described as "incurable" and "part of his genetic makeup." However, we are thankful to have a blood-bought, personal relationship with the Creator of Clemmie's body, and He is "not a God of disorder but of peace" (1 Corinthians 14:33 NLT). This truth began a further pursuit of our God's will for Clemmie, and He would grow our faith beyond what we could possibly imagine. I believe the Lord had already been building our faith to say *no* to being satisfied with the diagnosis and saying *yes* to walking "by faith, not by sight" (2 Corinthians 5:7).

Psalm 139:13–18 says, "For You formed my inward parts; You covered me in my mother's womb. I will praise You, for I am fearfully and wonderfully made; marvelous are Your works, and that my soul knows very well. My frame was not hidden from You, when I was made in secret, and skillfully wrought in the lowest parts of the earth. Your eyes saw my substance, being yet unformed. And in Your book they all were written, the days fashioned for me, when as yet there were none of them. How precious also are Your thoughts to me, O God! How great the sum of them! If I should count them, they would be more in number than the sand." I love this passage of Scripture. If there is ever a doubt of God's special purpose and design for *every* little baby in the womb, then read Psalm 139. I am in awe of how our God thinks so much of us. His thoughts toward us are too numerous to count. We were *all* created for a purpose.

WHY THE DELAY?

He sees us and has great plans for us.

I believe we can be completely convinced about how precious our God's thoughts are toward us, so let's dig a little deeper into the meaning of some of these words. The Hebrew word used for *formed* means *"to erect, create, procure, especially by purchase; by implication, to own, attain, possess, recover, and redeem."* This means that our heavenly Father, in His sovereignty, had already purchased and redeemed Clemmie before he was even born. That is truly exciting! Another exciting truth is that Clemmie was *"covered,"* which means *"to entwine as a screen, to fence in, cover over, protect, defend, hedge in, and join together."* With whom was Clem joined together? As Clemmie was being *redeemed* in my womb, our God was *protecting, defending, entwining as a screen*, and *joining him together* with *Himself*. How powerful is that? Before you were even born, and before the world found any value in you, the Lord God Almighty *heavily esteemed* you and found you to be *precious, valuable,* and *prized*. He *set you apart* and *made you different* from anyone else so that everyone would take notice and *reverently* stand in *awe* of His power and glory in you. The Master Potter *molded into form* and *gave purpose* to each of your days. You are not an accident. I am not an accident. Clemmie is not an accident. Each of us has purpose, and if we have made Jesus the Lord and Savior of our lives, He has been drawing us to Himself since before we were born. Dear friend, He is asking us to come in closer even now.

The Lord continued to confirm His Word, precept upon precept, to us as we sought Him. "I sought the Lord, and He heard me, and delivered me from all my fears" (Psalm 34:4). We were becoming confident in His promises, and our fears for Clemmie and his future were dimming "in the light of His glory and grace."[1] As we began opening our ears to hear God's voice, not relying on our carnal mind's understanding, we were directed to places and people who were bold in the Spirit of God and equipped to encourage us in our faith. We took Clemmie to other states. We drove hours to find faith-filled servants of YHWH-*Râphâ*—"the God who heals" (Exodus 15:26). These people believed the Word regarding healing. They were faithful warriors who truly believed that part of their Great Commission was to "lay hands on the sick, and they will recover" (Mark 16:18). We were desperate to find folks who walked in this kind of mountain-moving faith. Jesus said, "For assuredly, I say to you, if you have faith as a mustard seed, you will say to this mountain, 'Move from here to there,' and it will move; and *nothing* will be impossible for you'" (Matthew 17:20). In these meetings, we saw many instantly walk free of their oppressions, whether mental, emotional, or physical. However, the very first concern of these faithful prayer warriors was whether or not each one they prayed for had a personal relationship with God the Father through the sacrifice of Jesus Christ, the Son, and that we were walking in newness of life through the resurrecting power

---

[1] "The Heavenly Vision," also known as "Turn Your Eyes upon Jesus," written by Helen Howarth Lemmel in 1922. Based on Isaiah 45:22.

of the Holy Spirit. "It is the Spirit who gives life; the flesh profits nothing. The words I speak to you are spirit, and they are life" (John 6:63).

At every meeting we attended, Shad and I were asked about our personal relationships with Jesus. These people did not know us personally. They had not seen firsthand how we had lived out our lives for the Lord. It was only through the discernment of the Holy Spirit that they could see our hearts as they heard our testimonies. The point of their probes was to help us search deep in our hearts for any unconfessed sin. James 5:16 tells us to "confess your trespasses to one another, and pray for one another, that you may be healed." In order for us to be effective intercessors for our son, we needed to make sure there was nothing sinful hidden in us that needed to be revealed and uprooted. It was a time of self-examination for Shad and me. "Search me, O God, and know my heart. Examine me and know my anxious thoughts" (Psalm 139:23 TLV).

For some, it might seem insensitive to ask the parents of a young sick child if they have any unconfessed sins or anything from which they needed to be delivered. However, when you are desperate for salvation and healing, you take no offense. Desperation brings humility, and in true humility, there is no offense. Humility is where we find true healing. Look at Matthew's account of the Canaanite woman who comes to Jesus in desperation. "Have mercy on me, O Lord, Son of David! My daughter is demon-possessed" (Matthew 15:22). This was a Gentile woman who traveled to see the Jewish Savior, hoping for Him to show her mercy. Scripture says that she "cried out to Him." Was she willing to face humiliation for her daughter to receive healing? Absolutely! She persisted, even in the face of what looked to be rejection. Jesus remained silent and *waited*. The disciples wanted Jesus to turn her away. She came in further and "worshiped Him, saying, 'Lord help me!'" (Matthew 15:25). Was anything going to hinder this mother from receiving her daughter's healing? Jesus was willing, but He *waited*. Was she willing to truly die to self and give up every trace of pride to attain the healing? Without realizing it, this Canaanite woman's heart was being purified in the waiting, and evidence of what remained in her heart was about to be revealed to Jesus. Remember, inclusion of the Gentiles in God's redemptive plan had not yet been revealed to the disciples. Their focus was on the unsaved children of Israel. Matthew 15:26–28 in the *Tree of Life Version* says, "And answering, He said, 'It's not right to take the children's bread and throw it to the dogs.' But she said, 'Yes, Master, but even the dogs eat the crumbs that fall from their master's table.' Then answering, Yeshua said to her, 'O woman, great is your faith! Let it be done for you as you wish.' And her daughter was healed in that very hour." This desperate mother took no offense, but she was instead relentless in coming to the Savior. Even in the face of deep humiliation, her unyielding faith was greatly rewarded. Her daughter was healed.

How many of us would have remained after receiving

WHY THE DELAY?

no response from the Master? How many of us would've persisted in approaching the Healer after being compared to a dog? One might have the inclination to think it is not His will to heal *my* child and therefore leave in utter disgrace. Thankfully, Jesus did not view her in this manner, contrary to Jewish culture. Jesus knew that true faith in the Messiah would defy those insecurities. He also understood that the *disciples needed to witness faith* in action so they would understand the heart of the Father. "He is not willing that any should perish but that all should come to repentance" (2 Peter 3:9).

As we look through Scripture, we see several times when Jesus delayed in His response. His will was always to heal, but the healing did not always come at the exact moment those concerned thought it should come. Now, before we dig deeper into this, I want to make it clear that I believe that "all of God's promises have been fulfilled in Christ with a resounding 'Yes!' and through Christ, our 'Amen' (which means 'Yes') ascends to God for His glory" (2 Corinthians 1:20 NLT). I also believe the Word when it says, "I tell you, now is the time of God's favor, now is the day of salvation" (2 Corinthians 6:6 NIV). So, I believe healing has already been done through Jesus. The price for our freedom from sin *and* its penalty has been paid in full. It was finished at the cross. I pray you *believe* that, too, and *speak these truths* over whatever you are battling. *Expect* complete health and wholeness every day based on His promises in Christ Jesus and not on what you see or how you feel. *Stand firmly* on His Word.

However, the purpose of this lesson is to encourage us not to be disheartened if there is a delay in how quickly we *see* the full healing. Our God wants us to believe Him no matter what we see or feel. "And my righteous ones will live by faith. But I will take no pleasure in anyone who turns away" (Hebrews 10:38 NLT). The Greek word used for *faith* in this verse means "*convinced, certain, confidence, persuaded, trust, constancy in such profession,* and *assurance.*" Are we truly confident and convinced, making it our constant profession that Jesus is Healer, or are we not fully persuaded and sure that Jesus is the Healer? It grieves God's heart when we do not believe Him. In fact, when we *abstain, shrink back, cower under, conceal,* and *withdraw* from our conviction and profession of Him as Healer, in those who doubt He takes *no pleasure—does not approve, does not think good of, is not well-pleased,* and *is not willing.* In other words, "without faith it is impossible to please God" (Hebrews 11:6 TLV).

I've heard several explanations about why "Jesus wept" in John 11:35, and I believe Jesus wept because those closest to Him doubted. Jesus loved Mary, Martha, and their brother, Lazarus, but when the two sisters sent a message to Jesus that their brother was sick, Jesus delayed in coming to Lazarus. He delayed so long that Lazarus had been dead four days and was already buried. When questioned why He did not come to heal His friend right away, Jesus spoke clearly of the reason for His delay in

WHY THE DELAY?

John 11, verses 4, 15, and 42. The delay was for the glory of God and so that the Son of God would be glorified through his healing. Speaking to the disciples, Jesus said in John 11:15 (TLV), "I'm glad for your sake I wasn't there, so that you may believe." Look at how Jesus questioned Martha: "Didn't I tell you that you would see God's glory if you believe?" (John 11:40 NLT). He said this to Martha after she questioned why He didn't come sooner. She told Jesus that she believed her brother would be raised up in the last days. Her faith only took her as far as what she could see, and then it took her to what she believed about the last days. Martha did not trust that whenever Jesus came, no matter how long it took, Jesus would do as He promised. Finally, before He raised Lazarus up from death and the grave, Jesus said when praying to His Father, "I knew that You always hear Me; but because of this crowd standing around I said it, so that they may believe that You sent Me" (John 11:42 TLV). Notice this: Jesus never admonished Lazarus about *his* lack of faith. Jesus' delay had little to do with teaching Lazarus about faith, even though I'm sure Lazarus learned a lot. His delay, however, was to *convince* the two sisters, the disciples, and the crowd that He was the fulfillment of God's promise in order for God the Father and the Son to be glorified in Lazarus's healing. Jesus was teaching *faith* to the crowd witnessing the miracle. It was for *their* benefit and His glory.

There seems to be a common misunderstanding regarding those who battle *infirmity*. Similar to how the original twelve disciples believed in John 9, the body of Christ is quick to believe the *feeble, weak, diseased,* or *sick* person and his family sinned in some way to result in the sickness. I cannot count how many times Shad and I have been asked if there is sin in our own lives that might have caused Clem to battle what he is battling—and that is okay, because every believer should be looking inwardly at where he or she needs cleansing. While there are many who are sick because of their disobedience and lack of self-control, there are those who, through no fault of their own and for whatever reason, are born with their infirmities. I believe, similar to what Jesus said and did with the blind man in John 9, the Lord wants to gather the multitudes to bear witness to His signs and wonders, just as He did with Lazarus and his two sisters. Of course, in the waiting there is always something to be learned about our God and His heart.

Waiting also reveals what is hidden in our hearts. Exposed in the waiting is how much we trust our heavenly Father. The refining in the waiting can purge anything that hinders us from an intimate relationship with the One True God. We have the choice to believe Him through His Word or reject His words. Shad and I continue to *search* the deepest parts of our hearts every day to prevent any stronghold from hindering our faith from becoming sight, but we truly believe God each day for those signs and wonders to be revealed in Clemmie. So, why the delay in seeing what we have prayed for and believed? Or do we

WHY THE DELAY?

see glimpses of his healing every day? "Now faith is the substance of things hoped for, the evidence of realities not seen" (Hebrews 11:1 TLV). Are our spiritual eyes open to see the "evidence of realities not seen"? Are we looking and expecting God to accomplish in Clemmie what He has promised in His Word?

Think of all the people who waited years to receive healing from the Messiah. The woman with the issue of blood *waited* twelve years to glorify the Lord through her healing, in Matthew 9:20–22. The paralytic *waited* thirty-eight years to walk into his healing, in John 5:1–8. The synagogue leader whose daughter had died still came to Jesus believing that His touch would bring her back to life. Even while on their way to his house, the ruler had to *wait* until Jesus healed the woman with the issue of blood before Jesus reached his daughter. He *waited* as Jesus took His time emptying the house of grieving, wailing, and unbelieving people before He went in, took the girl's hand, and raised her up out of that bed. Imagine the patience of this daddy. His forbearance was due to the *confidence* he had in the Savior's plans. I'm sure the words from the prophet Jeremiah came to mind as he waited in full assurance of what the Lord would do. Jeremiah 29:11 (TLV) says this: "'For I know the plans I have in mind for you,' declares Adonai, 'plans for shalom and not calamity—to give you a future and a hope.'" Are we as confident in our Lord's promises as he was? These Scriptures are just some of the stories of those who waited to receive their healing from the Promised One sent to save and heal. The difference between us and them is this: we have the written accounts in the New Testament of Jesus fulfilling the will of the Father by healing *all* who were sick with various diseases "to fulfill what was spoken through the prophet Isaiah: 'He took up our infirmities and bore our diseases'" (Matthew 8:16 NIV). We also have the *finished work* at the cross. The spotless Lamb of God died and then was raised up from that death so that we might live life to the fullest (John 10:10). So, what excuse do we have not to believe His promises in doing His will "on earth as it is in heaven" (Matthew 6:10 TLV)? I believe He is gathering the crowds to show His signs and wonders through His Church, and He is waiting until we are desperate for Him and nothing else.

Through story after story, healing after healing, we see the Father's will revealed in the works of Jesus. In Matthew 17:14–21, Mark 9:17–29, and Luke 9:37–43, we see Jesus' response when the father of the boy with seizures asked Jesus to heal his son. Jesus first admonished those around Him: "Where is your faith? Can't you see how wayward and wrong this generation is? How much longer do I stay with you and put up with your doubts? Bring your son to me" (Matthew 17:17 TPT). As I meditate on this verse, my prayer is that I never hear those words from my Jesus. I don't want Him to question my faith. I do believe, Lord! Help my unbelief! Jesus cast the demon out, and the boy was instantly healed. The disciples were confused as to why they could not cast out this "mute and dumb spirit." Jesus told them it was because of their lack of faith. If they only had faith the size of a mustard seed, nothing would be impossible for them to do. Additionally, this mute and dumb spirit must also be cast out "through prayer and fasting" (verse 21). I am so thankful to have this example in Scripture of what needed to be done to heal the epileptic. Jesus lived a life of prayer and fasting. He was equipped and ready to meet every need, not because He was fully God, but rather because He was fully surrendered to His Father's will. Like the disciples, Jesus was fully human. The difference was trust and complete dedication to doing the will of Adonai. Jesus was not only the complete sacrifice for us, but He lived life completely sacrificing His flesh daily. What if we were to live as living sacrifices as Jesus did? In 2005, I began living a life with times of fasting and prayer on behalf of my son. Twenty years later, I still set aside times to fast as I pray. I have seen signs of healing in Clemmie, but I have also witnessed the enemy's relentless attacks. There have been times of joy and times of sorrow. There have been times of rest, and there have been sleepless nights. Through it all, we have remained steadfast in trusting Jesus as Clemmie's Healer. In the words of my wise husband, "We're in the weeds at ground level, and we do not fully see how Clem's healing has *already* been revealed in him." The evidence is there. Do we have eyes to see?

I've found myself wishing that I could physically

approach Jesus just as this boy's daddy did, and just as others did who were desperate to see their healing. Then the Holy Spirit reminds me, *You can*. Friend, we are the hands and feet of Jesus. Jesus' own words—"How much longer do I stay with you and put up with your doubts?"—is evidence enough that He fully expects us to *believe* as He did and *do* as He did. Are we vessels the Holy Spirit works through to bring about someone's healing, or are we stumbling blocks who cause someone to doubt? Jesus promises in John 14:12 (NIV) that "whoever believes in Me will do the works I have been doing, and they will do even greater things than these, because I am going to the Father." That is a pretty significant promise! Greater works than Jesus? How? Jesus tells us we have a Helper, the Holy Spirit, and there is no greater power in the world (1 John 4:4).

So, why the delay? First of all, it is my experience that waiting creates a longing for our heavenly home and an eternal outlook of the purpose for our lives here on earth. When we have an eternal perspective, we are less likely to "store up treasures on earth" (Matthew 6:19). Everything we say and do will have eternal value and bring the Lord Jesus praise. Second, why not? Why not grow deeper in the waiting? Why not come to the end of ourselves and desperately lay at His feet in order for our faithful Father to reveal exactly who He is? And finally, why not gather the crowds in the waiting? Why not let them see how deeply we trust Him to fulfill all that He has promised? First

Thessalonians 5:24 (TLV) says, "Faithful is the One who calls you—and He will make it happen!" Point others to the promises in His Word. Remember His faithfulness to fulfill His promises from generation to generation. Moses waited forty years. Joseph waited thirteen years. Noah waited one hundred years. Abraham waited twenty-five years. Jesus waited thirty years. So, we're in good company when we wait patiently on the Lord. The value of waiting far exceeds the value of instant relief from our troubles. Will we bless Him while we wait, or will we doubt His faithfulness?

Waiting creates deeper roots, and deeper roots keep us firmly planted during the violent storms of life. People will notice. "The Lord is not slow in keeping His promise, as some consider slowness. Rather, He is being patient toward you—not wanting anyone to perish, but for all to come to repentance" (2 Peter 3:9 TLV). Think of the people who will see our faith in the One who is faithful. Testify and stand amazed in His presence. The lost will seek the Shelter we abide under, and the saved will come in a little closer. If just one person comes to repentance and salvation through Jesus Christ because of our perseverance through this trial, it will be worth it all. That is the eternal outlook we have as a result of the delay, "and not only that, but we also boast in suffering—knowing that suffering produces perseverance; and perseverance, character; and character, hope. And hope does not disappoint, because God's love has poured into our hearts through the Holy Spirit[2] who was given to

---

2 Romans 5:3–5, *Tree of Life* translation, *Ruach ha-Kodesh*.

us" (Romans 5:3–5 TLV). No matter how long it takes to see what God has promised, press on and endure to see its completion, knowing that He who promised is faithful (Hebrews 10:23).

Revelation: It is in the waiting that we use our faith muscles to become stronger in trusting our Lord and Savior. The delay builds endurance, which builds character. Our character becomes His character. In the waiting, we are transformed into the image of His dear Son.

… WHY THE DELAY?

WRITE DOWN WHAT THE HOLY SPIRIT SAYS TO YOU:

Afterword

Dearest reader, if you get nothing else from reading these stories, I pray you will understand the authority and power you have been given through the Spirit of the living God. If we understand who lives within us, and how deeply He wants to do greater things in and through us, nothing will be impossible. In this world, we will have triumphs, and we will have trials. We will have moments at the top of the mountain, and we will have moments down in the valley. There will be times when we will be full of excitement and celebration, ready to conquer what is ahead of us, but there will also be times when we feel weary and fatigued, thinking we have very little left to move forward. This is when it *feels so good to lay down*. Lay down and rest, knowing He is able to take all your burdens, all your cares, and all your moments of weakness to create a more sanctified and complete vessel for His glory. Let Him be your strength and song (Psalm 118:14). Allow His strength to be made perfect in weakness (2 Corinthians 12:9). It is in our weakest moments where we can truly find rest. When we realize we have nothing more to give, we bow low in humility and let Him fill us with an overflow to bless and encourage others. "Therefore, humble yourselves under the mighty hand of God, so that He may lift you up at the appropriate time. Cast all your worries on Him, for He cares for you" (1 Peter 5:6–7 TLV).

Know this, beloved: our heavenly Father deeply cares for you. You are the apple of His eye. He will do as He has promised—I have no doubt! I want you to be confident of His faithfulness, too. Know Him more. Rest in His goodness and faithfulness to all generations. Listen to Him speak to you. Be still and let Him sing over you to calm all of your fears. Give Him every part of you and allow Him to give you His peace. Lay it all down and lay down in complete surrender to His power and mighty hand. He will lift you up at the right time, knowing exactly the time that is best for your consecration and His exaltation. In Jesus' name. Amen.

Glossary of Transliterations

Lesson 3	It's All a Matter of Perspective *Redeemed* Strong's #h1350
Lesson 9	"Get in Here Now" *Run* Strong's #h7323
Lesson 18	"Mom, You're Beautiful" *Delight* Strong's #h2656
Lesson 20	The "Shade-y" Choice *Fornication* Strong's #g4202, g4203, g4204 *Idolatry* Strong's #g1495, g1497, g2999
Lesson 24	It's Not a "Kai-peeper!" *Repentance* Strong's #g3341, g3340
Lesson 27	Pick Up Trash or Pick Flowers… Your Choice *Without form* Strong's #h8414

Lesson 29	The Pathway Cleared	
	Direct	Strong's #h3474
	Paths	Strong's #h734, h732
	Leads	Strong's #h5148
	Paths	Strong's #h4570, h5696
	Righteousness	Strong's #h6664, h6663
	For sake	Strong's #h4616, h6030
	His name	Strong's #h8034, h7760
Lesson 30	Put Him Down	
	Peace	Strong's #g1515
	Whole/Healed	Strong's #h7495
Lesson 31	"Life is Like A Popcorn Toot"	
	Abide	Strong's #g3306
Lesson 32	Preparing the Soil	
	Wayside	Strong's #g3598
Lesson 35	Brother's Keeper	
	Adversity	Strong's #h6869
	Born	Strong's #h3205
	Rule	Strong's #h4910
	Keeper	Strong's #h8104
Lesson 36	Overlooking the Heart of God	
	Diligent	Strong's #g4704
	Present	Strong's #g3936
	Approved	Strong's #g1384

GLOSSARY OF TRANSLITERATIONS

Worker	Strong's #g2040
Ashamed	Strong's #g422
Rightly Dividing	Strong's #g3718
Word	Strong's #g3056
Amazed	Strong's #g2296
Pour out	Strong's #g1632, g1537
Commend	Strong's #g4921
Servant	Strong's #g1249
Receive	Strong's #g4327
Assist	Strong's #g3936
Greet	Strong's #g782
Labored	Strong's #g2872
Judge	Strong's #g2919

Lesson 37   The Joy of Disentanglement
- *Nissî*   Strong's #h3071
- *Joy*   Strong's #h2304

Lesson 38   Growth Spurts
- *Fear*   Strong's #h3374, h3373, h3372

Lesson 39   A "Chord" of Three Strands
- *Three*   Strong's #h7969, 7991, 8027
- *Midst*   Strong's #g3319

Lesson 40   The Delay
- *Formed*   Strong's #h7069
- *Covered*   Strong's #h5526

Fearfully	Strong's #h3372
Wonderfully	Strong's #h6395
Fashioned	Strong's #h3335
Precious	Strong's #h3365
Heals	Strong's #h7495
Faith	Strong's #g4102
Turns Away	Strong's #g5288
No Pleasure	Strong's #g2106
Infirmities	Strong's #g769

About the Author

Tiffany Haynes Vinson is a third-generation minister of the Gospel, former military spouse, and mother of a child with special needs. She began music ministry at a young age and went on to further her education in music at the University of North Texas, where she met her husband, Shad. Shad was commissioned into the Air Force upon graduation from UNT, and they married seven months later. Shad and Tiffany spent twenty years as an active-duty military family, with military assignments in California, Oklahoma, and Maryland before Shad's retirement in 2017. They now live back home in Texas with their two boys, Clemmie and Colt. Tiffany is passionate about the Word of God, music evangelism, the Church, and special-needs families.

Printed in the USA
CPSIA information can be obtained
at www.ICGtesting.com
CBHW071919090924
14064CB00008B/113